Religions Around the World:

Exploring the Beliefs of the 12 Major Faiths

DAVID M. EATON

Contents

Introduction

A Journey into the Heart of Global Spirituality

Throughout human history, there has been beliefs that span cultures, continents, and centuries. Many that still exist today. These beliefs are the essence of our quest for meaning, purpose, and connection to the mysteries of existence. Everyone has their own specific belief that gives them faith and comfort in hard times.

From the ancient rituals of indigenous tribes to the soaring cathedrals of Christianity, from the tranquil gardens of Buddhism to the call for prayer of Islam, humanity's spiritual journey is a vibrant mosaic, woven with the diverse strands of faith that bind us together as humans.

For as long as the world has been turning, religion has been a subject of interest. No matter what your particular faith, learning about other religions around the world is a way to understand other people and expand your mind. Welcome to "Religions Around the World: Exploring the Beliefs of the 12 Major Faiths," an exploration of the breath-taking diversity and profound unity that define our global spiritual landscape.

The idea isn't to change your own beliefs or pull apart anyone else's. Instead, it's to understand and embrace differences in beliefs. Through true understanding comes tolerance, and perhaps even peace.

Diversity in Global Religions

As people move around the world from country to country, their beliefs begin to intertwine, overlap, and interact with unprecedented intensity. This fact gives rise to a remarkable phenomenon—the convergence of cultures and faiths that prompts us to re-evaluate our understanding of religious diversity. It's an opportunity to see the world through a different lens. The symphony of chants, prayers, and hymns that rise from every corner of the world concurs with the enduring human need for answers to the age-old questions of existence, and it beckons us to embark on a journey that traverses both the external and internal landscapes of belief.

The Importance of Understanding Different Belief Systems

Understanding different belief systems becomes not only a privilege but a necessity. The importance of appreciating the intricacies of each faith cannot be overstated. From fostering empathy and promoting peaceful coexistence to thwarting the misperceptions that lead to conflict, understanding different belief systems is the linchpin of a harmonious global society.

In-depth knowledge of religious narratives dispels the clouds of ignorance, allowing us to see the shared humanity that underlies the diversity of practices and rituals. When we realize that the prayers whispered in a temple, the songs sung in a church, and the rituals performed in a mosque all resonate with the universal aspirations of the human heart, we awaken to a common language that transcends boundaries and brings us closer together.

Religion doesn't have to pull people apart; it's very aim is to unite.

An Invitation to Understanding and Unity

As you move through the coming chapters and embark on journey of discovery, prepare to traverse continents and epochs, to encounter practices both familiar and foreign, and to unveil the shared aspirations that bind us as a global community. The goal is not to dilute the uniqueness of each faith, but to magnify the universal truths that they collectively express—the desire to understand, to connect, and to seek meaning in a world where the tapestry of belief is as intricate as the human soul itself.

This book invites you to not merely read about these beliefs, but to embark on a personal pilgrimage, guided by curiosity, respect, and a profound desire to learn from the stories that have shaped countless lives. So, let us begin our journey to empathy, understanding, and the timeless quest for a greater connection to the world within and around us.

Chapter 1

Hinduism

In human spirituality, Hinduism contains vibrant threads of mythology, philosophy, and diverse cultural expressions. Rooted in the ancient lands of the Indian subcontinent, Hinduism has nurtured a profound relationship between the divine and the mortal, offering seekers a kaleidoscope of beliefs that mirror the complexities of existence.

From the majestic stories of gods and goddesses to the intricate philosophies of karma and moksha, Hinduism paints a portrait of the human journey—exploring the cosmos both within and beyond.

Hinduism: The Ancient Fabric of Spirituality

Few traditions possess the timeless depth and intricate diversity of Hinduism. Emerging from ancient India, this profound belief system has woven itself into the very fabric of the subcontinent's history, culture, and identity. As we delve into the origins and historical development of Hinduism, we embark on a journey through millennia—a journey that uncovers not only the evolution of a religion but also the evolution of a way of life.

Origins: The Dawn of Spiritual Thought

The origins of Hinduism are shrouded in the mists of antiquity, stretching back thousands of years to the earliest civilizations that flourished along the banks of the Indus and Saraswati rivers. The Vedas, a collection of ancient scriptures, serve as the foundational texts of this faith, capturing the insights and spiritual inquiries of ancient seers and sages. These texts, written in Sanskrit, reveal the early stages of a profound philosophical exploration into the nature of reality, the cosmos, and the divine.

Through centuries, Hinduism evolved into a diverse and multi-faceted belief system, with its teachings embracing an astonishing array of philosophies, rituals, and practices. It is a religion that defies easy categorization, as it welcomes a multitude of perspectives and interpretations.

One of the key developments in the historical evolution of Hinduism was the emergence of philosophical schools known as darshanas. These schools, including Vedanta, Nyaya, and Samkhya, explored intricate questions about the nature of existence, the relationship between the individual soul (atman) and the universal soul (Brahman), and the paths to spiritual liberation (moksha). Each darshana offered a unique lens through which devotees could contemplate the mysteries of life.

The concept of dharma, a central pillar of Hinduism, emerged as a guiding principle for ethical and moral conduct. Dharma encompasses duty, righteousness, and the observance of social responsibilities, reflecting the belief that living in harmony with your role and responsibilities contributes to a balanced and just society.

As the centuries unfolded, Hinduism absorbed and synthesized various influences from neighboring cultures and traditions. The rise of devotional movements introduced the concept of bhakti, emphasizing a personal and heartfelt connection with the divine. The epics, Ramayana and Mahabharata, further enriched the Hindu narrative with legendary stories, allegories, and ethical dilemmas that continue to inspire millions.

Unity in Diversity: The Enduring Essence

What is most striking about Hinduism's historical development is its ability to accommodate an astonishing diversity of beliefs and practices while maintaining a core unity. From the worship of countless deities—Vishnu, Shiva, Devi, and more—to the reverence for sacred texts like the Bhagavad Gita, the Ramayana, and the Upanishads, Hindus find a myriad of paths to connect with the divine.

Hinduism's fluidity has allowed it to adapt to changing times while remaining anchored in its ancient roots. Its concepts of karma (the law of cause and effect) and reincarnation (the cycle of birth, death, and rebirth) have offered solace and guidance, reflecting the profound understanding that each life is a step on the journey toward self-realization and ultimate liberation.

The origins and historical development of Hinduism reveal a religion that has grown, evolved, and flourished over millennia. From its humble beginnings in the Vedic era to its multifaceted modern expression, Hinduism stands as a testament to the enduring power of spiritual inquiry and the ability to encompass a rich tapestry of beliefs, practices, and philosophies. As we delve deeper into the beliefs and practices of Hinduism, we uncover a tradition that continues to inspire and shape the lives of millions with its wisdom, beauty, and timeless teachings.

Core Beliefs of Hinduism: Dharma, Karma, and Moksha

Hinduism is a profound and intricate belief system. Among these beliefs, three stand out prominently: Dharma, Karma, and Moksha. These concepts not only shape the moral compass of Hindu followers but also offer profound philosophical insights that have intrigued scholars and seekers for centuries.

Dharma: The Cosmic Order and Moral Duty

At the heart of Hinduism lies the concept of dharma—an intricate and dynamic force that encompasses the ethical and moral order of the universe. Dharma reflects the cosmic harmony and balance that underpins existence. In simple terms, it guides individuals in recognizing and fulfilling their roles, responsibilities, and obligations within society, family, and life itself.

Dharma is not a static concept but rather adapts to different contexts, roles, and stages of life. It emphasizes living ethically and virtuously, upholding righteousness and justice, and contributing positively to the well-being of society. Dharma also embodies the idea of selfless service, reminding individuals that the pursuit of personal gain should never come at the expense of others. It is through the fulfillment of one's dharma that a person contributes to the collective equilibrium of the world.

Karma: The Law of Cause and Effect

Central to Hinduism's understanding of human existence is the principle of karma—the law of cause and effect that governs the consequences of one's actions. According to this belief, every action, thought, and intention sets into motion a chain of events. Positive actions lead to positive outcomes, while negative actions result in negative consequences.

Karma is not only about reward and punishment; it is also about spiritual growth and self-realization. Through the cycle of karma, individuals have the opportunity to learn and evolve, progressing toward a higher state of consciousness. This concept encourages mindfulness and ethical behavior, as individuals are reminded that their actions have far-reaching implications beyond the here and now.

Moksha: Liberation and Spiritual Fulfillment

Moksha, often referred to as liberation or enlightenment, represents the ultimate goal of human life according to Hinduism. It is the state of transcending the cycle of birth, death, and rebirth (samsara) and achieving union with the divine or realization of the true self (atman). Moksha is the culmination of a spiritual journey that involves self-discovery, detachment from material desires, and the pursuit of higher knowledge.

The paths to moksha are manifold, reflecting the diversity within Hinduism. Some seek liberation through the path of devotion (bhakti), immersing themselves in worship and surrendering to the divine. Others pursue the path of knowledge (jnana), engaging in philosophical contemplation and meditation to attain self-realization. The path of disciplined action (karma yoga) emphasizes selfless service as a means to purify the mind and transcend ego.

The core beliefs of Hinduism—Dharma, Karma, and Moksha—form an intricate web of interconnected concepts. These beliefs inspire individuals to live with purpose, to embrace ethical conduct, and to embark on a journey toward liberation.

Together, they provide a roadmap for navigating life's complexities while striving for a deeper understanding of your place in the cosmos and the ultimate realization of the divine within.

Deities and Pantheon: Brahma, Vishnu, Shiva

Among the most prominent and revered are the trinity of deities: Brahma, Vishnu, and Shiva. These three divine beings, known as the Trimurti, play integral roles in shaping the universe, maintaining cosmic order, and guiding the spiritual journey of devotees.

Brahma: The Creator

Brahma is often seen as the creator of the universe, responsible for existence from chaos. While Brahma is one of the principal deities, he is less commonly worshiped compared to Vishnu and Shiva.

In Hindu iconography, Brahma is often depicted with four heads symbolizing the four Vedas, the sacred texts of Hinduism. His four arms hold a rosary, a water vessel, a book of knowledge, and a lotus, signifying creation, purification, wisdom, and beauty.

While Brahma's role in creation is celebrated, his limited presence in Hindu mythology and worship reflects the belief that creation is an ongoing process that doesn't require continuous intervention. Instead, Brahma's significance lies in the initial spark of creation that set the universe in motion.

Vishnu: The Preserver

Vishnu, one of the most revered deities in Hinduism, is the preserver of the universe and the embodiment of divine order (dharma). Vishnu is often depicted in a serene manner, reclining on the cosmic serpent Ananta, while he rests on the celestial waters. His role is to maintain balance and harmony in the universe, intervening whenever chaos threatens to disrupt cosmic equilibrium.

Vishnu's incarnations (avatars) are a key aspect of his worship. The most famous of these avatars is Lord Rama, who embodies righteousness and duty, and Lord Krishna, known for his divine playfulness and the teachings of the Bhagavad Gita. Vishnu's worshippers seek his grace and protection, believing that through devotion and righteous living, they can maintain a connection with the divine and fulfill their dharma.

Shiva: The Destroyer and Transformer

Shiva, often depicted in meditation or performing the cosmic dance of destruction (Tandava), is both the destroyer and the regenerator of the universe. His role is to dissolve the old and make way for the new, symbolizing the cyclical nature of existence. Shiva is associated with asceticism, meditation, and the yogic path. His third eye represents inner vision and insight, capable of both destruction and enlightenment.

Shiva's devotees seek his blessings for spiritual growth, inner transformation, and liberation from the cycle of birth and death. His consort, Parvati, embodies the divine feminine and represents Shakti—the cosmic energy that animates creation. Together, they symbolize the union of opposites and the balance between creation and destruction.

Thus, Brahma, Vishnu, and Shiva form a triad of deities that together represent the cosmic cycle of creation, preservation, and destruction. Their distinct roles reflect the multifaceted nature of existence and offer a framework for understanding the divine forces that shape the universe. By engaging with these deities, Hindus connect with the profound principles that guide their spiritual journey and illuminate the mysteries of the cosmos.

Practices and Rituals in Hinduism: Yoga, Meditation, and Festivals

Hinduism is a living tapestry of practices and rituals that span the spectrum from deeply personal acts of devotion to grand communal celebrations. These practices are not only a means of connecting with the divine but also a way of embodying spiritual principles and fostering a sense of community. Among the diverse array of practices and rituals, three stand out prominently: yoga, meditation, and festivals.

Yoga: Union of Body, Mind, and Spirit

Yoga, derived from the Sanskrit word "yuj," meaning to unite or join, is a holistic system that seeks to harmonize the body, mind, and spirit. Beyond exercise, yoga is deeply rooted in Hindu philosophy and is a spiritual practice with profound implications. It offers various paths to self-realization, including:

1. **Raja Yoga**: Focuses on meditation and mental discipline to achieve self-mastery.
2. **Karma Yoga**: Emphasizes selfless service and ethical action as a means to spiritual growth.
3. **Bhakti Yoga**: Centers on devotion and love for the divine, fostering an emotional connection.
4. **Jnana Yoga**: Involves the pursuit of knowledge and philosophical inquiry to attain self-realization.

Through these paths, yoga enables practitioners to transcend the limitations of the ego and connect with the divine essence within.

Meditation: Journey Inward

Meditation is another integral practice in Hinduism, aimed at quietening the mind and achieving inner clarity. Meditation techniques vary, ranging from mindfulness to mantra repetition, but they all share the goal of facilitating self-awareness and insight. Meditation is seen as a means to access deeper states of consciousness, commune with the divine, and experience profound peace and contentment. It allows individuals to go beyond the constant chatter of the mind and tap into a wellspring of tranquility and inner wisdom.

Festivals: Celebrating the Divine

Hindu festivals are vibrant and colorful celebrations within the religious calendar, connecting communities and individuals with their spiritual roots. These festivals reflect the diversity of Hinduism and provide opportunities for devotion, cultural expression, and communal bonding. Some notable festivals include:

1. **Diwali (Deepavali)**: Known as the Festival of Lights, Diwali celebrates the triumph of light over darkness and good over evil. It involves lighting lamps, exchanging gifts, and feasting.
2. **Holi**: The Festival of Colors marks the arrival of spring and celebrates joy, love, and unity. People playfully throw colored powders and water at each other.
3. **Navaratri**: A nine-night festival dedicated to the goddess Durga, Navaratri involves dance, music, and fasting as devotees honor the divine feminine.

These festivals serve as reminders of the cyclical nature of life, the importance of rituals, and the connection between the individual and the cosmic.

The Influence of Hinduism on Culture and Society

Hinduism has exerted a profound influence on the cultures and societies of the Indian subcontinent and beyond. Its beliefs, practices, and philosophies has shaped everything from art and literature to social norms and governance. The influence of Hinduism on culture and society is vast and multifaceted, reflecting its deep integration into the fabric of life.

Art and Architecture: Manifestations of the Divine

Hinduism's influence is vividly evident in the art and architecture of the Indian subcontinent. Elaborate temples, adorned with intricate carvings and sculptures, serve as spaces for worship and contemplation. These architectural marvels reflect Hindu cosmology and mythology, depicting gods, goddesses, and stories from sacred texts.

The sculptures and paintings that adorn these structures are not merely decorative; they are powerful tools for conveying spiritual teachings and evoking devotion.

Literature and Philosophy: Seeds of Wisdom

Hinduism's philosophical underpinnings have impacted the literary and philosophical landscape. The Vedas, Upanishads, and epics like the Mahabharata and Ramayana inspired poets, scholars, and thinkers. The philosophical concepts of dharma, karma, and moksha have influenced not only spiritual thought but also discussions on ethics, morality, and the purpose of life.

The Bhagavad Gita, a philosophical dialogue set within the Mahabharata, offers guidance on duty, righteousness, and self-realization. Its teachings on detachment and selfless action resonate beyond the spiritual realm, influencing discussions on leadership, decision-making, and personal growth.

Social Norms and Practices: The Labyrinth of Tradition

Hinduism's influence extends to the realm of social norms and practices. The caste system, although often criticized for its rigidity, can be traced back to the ancient Vedic society. While this system has evolved over time, its influence is still visible in aspects of social structure and interaction.

Additionally, Hinduism's emphasis on dharma, karma, and the pursuit of righteousness has contributed to a complex set of moral guidelines that guide behavior and relationships. These principles have played a role in shaping societal norms related to duty, honor, and integrity.

Festivals and Celebrations: Weaving Unity

Hindu festivals are a testament to the religion's profound influence on community and cultural cohesion. Festivals like Diwali, Holi, and Navaratri bring people together, transcending differences of caste, class, and background. These celebrations foster a sense of belonging and unity, allowing diverse communities to share in a collective experience of devotion and celebration.

An Enduring Legacy

Hinduism's influence on culture and society is a testament to its enduring legacy. From the ancient temples that stand as testaments to spiritual devotion and the philosophical teachings that continue to guide human thought, Hinduism's impact is as diverse as the belief system itself. It has shaped art, literature, governance, and social norms, leaving an indelible mark on the civilizations that have flourished under its influence.

As societies continue to evolve, Hinduism's teachings and traditions remain an integral part of the ever-changing tapestry of human culture.

Chapter 2

Buddhism

Buddhism is a tranquil oasis, offering individuals a profound journey toward understanding the nature of existence and the quest for inner harmony. Born from the contemplative musings of Siddhartha Gautama, Buddhism has gently carved a path that traverses the complexities of human suffering, leading toward the serene shores of enlightenment.

With its teachings of impermanence, compassion, and the art of mindful living, Buddhism has captivated hearts and minds across the ages, transcending cultures and borders. As we begin to explore Buddhism, we immerse ourselves in the wisdom of the Four Noble Truths and the transformative Eightfold Path, resonating with the essence of a philosophy that beckons us to explore the depths of our own consciousness.

The Life of Siddhartha Gautama (Buddha): A Journey from Prince to Enlightened Sage

The life of Siddhartha Gautama, known to the world as the Buddha, is a profound story of spiritual awakening. His journey from a sheltered prince to an enlightened sage is a timeless narrative that continues to inspire seekers of truth and enlightenment.

Siddhartha Gautama was born in the 6th century BCE in the ancient kingdom of Kapilavastu, located in present-day Nepal. Born into royalty as the son of King Suddhodana and Queen Maya, Siddhartha was destined for a life of luxury and privilege. His birth was accompanied by auspicious signs and prophecies, foretelling that he would either become a great king or a spiritual leader who would liberate humanity from suffering.

Despite the opulence that surrounded him, Siddhartha's curiosity led him to explore the world beyond the palace walls. It was during these journeys that he encountered what are known as the "Four Sights": an old person, a sick person, a deceased person, and a wandering ascetic. These encounters shattered his illusion of perpetual happiness and exposed him to the harsh realities of human suffering, disease, and mortality.

Moved by the sights of suffering, Siddhartha made a momentous decision—to renounce his royal life in pursuit of spiritual truth and liberation. At the age of 29, he left behind his princely comforts, his wife, and infant son, and embarked on a life of asceticism. He studied under renowned teachers, seeking the ultimate answers to the questions that had consumed him since his encounters with suffering.

After years of rigorous ascetic practices, Siddhartha realized that extreme austerity was not the path to enlightenment. He embraced what he called the Middle Way—a balanced approach that avoided both self-indulgence and self-mortification. He embarked on a period of intense meditation, seeking answers to the nature of existence, suffering, and liberation.

Legend has it that at the age of 35, Siddhartha sat beneath the Bodhi tree in Bodh Gaya, India, determined to remain in meditation until he found the truth. After days of deep contemplation, he experienced a profound insight that revealed the nature of suffering and the path to liberation. This moment of realization marked his enlightenment, and he became known as the Buddha, meaning "the awakened one."

Following his enlightenment, the Buddha dedicated the remainder of his life to sharing his insights and teachings with the world. He wandered across ancient India, delivering information that later became the foundational texts of Buddhism—the Dhamma or Dharma. He explained the Four Noble Truths, which diagnose the nature of suffering and prescribe the Eightfold Path as a means to overcome it. He emphasized compassion, mindfulness, and ethical conduct as essential components of the spiritual journey.

After years of teaching and spreading his message, the Buddha passed away at the age of 80 in Kushinagar, India. He entered a state known as Parinirvana, marking his final release from the cycle of birth and death (samsara). His passing left behind a legacy of wisdom and compassion that has continued to guide countless people on the path to self-realization and liberation from suffering.

The Four Noble Truths and Eightfold Path: The Foundations of Buddhist Wisdom

At the heart of Buddhism, a profound philosophy and way of life, stand the Four Noble Truths and the Eightfold Path. These teachings form the core of Buddhist wisdom, offering a comprehensive framework for understanding the nature of suffering and the path to liberation.

The Four Noble Truths: The Diagnosis of Suffering

1. **Dukkha (Suffering)**: The first truth acknowledges the reality of suffering in human existence. This suffering, referred to as dukkha, encompasses not only physical pain but also the broader sense of dissatisfaction, impermanence, and the existential unease that pervades life.

2. **Samudaya (Origin)**: The second truth delves into the causes of suffering. It identifies attachment, craving, and ignorance as the roots of suffering. Attachment to desires, aversion to unpleasant experiences, and the delusion of permanence are highlighted as the sources of our discontent.

3. **Nirodha (Cessation)**: The third truth offers hope by proclaiming that suffering can be overcome. Nirodha, or cessation, is the end of craving, attachment, and ignorance. It is the possibility of liberation from the cycle of suffering and rebirth.

4. **Magga (Path)**: The fourth truth presents the path to liberation. The Eightfold Path is outlined as the means to achieve the cessation of suffering and attain enlightenment.

The Eightfold Path: The Journey to Enlightenment

The Eightfold Path provides a detailed roadmap for leading a life of ethical conduct, mental development, and wisdom. It is divided into three categories, often referred to as the three trainings:

1. Sila (Ethical Conduct):

- **Right Speech**: Avoiding lies, divisive speech, harsh speech, and idle chatter.

- **Right Action**: Abstaining from harming other people, stealing, and sexual misconduct.

- **Right Livelihood**: Engaging in an occupation that is honorable and non-harmful.

2. Samadhi (Mental Development):

- **Right Effort**: Cultivating a wholesome state of mind and eliminating unwholesome states.
- **Right Mindfulness**: Developing awareness of bodily sensations, feelings, thoughts, and mental states.
- **Right Concentration**: Cultivating a focused and tranquil state of mind through meditation.

3. Panna (Wisdom):

- **Right View**: Developing a correct understanding of the nature of reality, impermanence, and the Four Noble Truths.
- **Right Intention**: Cultivating intentions of renunciation, non-ill will, and non-harm.

The Eightfold Path is an interconnected web of practices that support one another. By cultivating ethical conduct, mental development, and wisdom, individuals navigate the complexities of life and gradually transcend the root causes of suffering.

Theravada, Mahayana, and Vajrayana: Exploring the Branches of Buddhism

Buddhism, with its rich and diverse philosophical landscape, has branched into several distinct traditions, each offering unique perspectives and practices. Three major branches—Theravada, Mahayana, and Vajrayana—emerge as primary expressions of Buddhist thought and practice, reflecting the evolution and adaptation of the teachings of Siddhartha Gautama, the Buddha.

Theravada Buddhism: The Way of the Elders

Theravada, often referred to as the "Way of the Elders," is considered one of the earliest and most conservative forms of Buddhism. It is common in countries such as Sri Lanka, Thailand, Myanmar, Cambodia, and Laos. Theravada adheres closely to the original teachings of the Buddha, as preserved in the Pali Canon—the collection of scriptures in the Pali language.

Key tenets of Theravada Buddhism include the Four Noble Truths, the Eightfold Path, and the concept of individual liberation through personal practice and self-discipline. Monasticism holds a central role in Theravada, and monks and nuns follow a strict code of conduct as they strive for enlightenment.

Mahayana Buddhism: The Great Vehicle

Mahayana, often translated as the "Great Vehicle," emerged later as a more inclusive and expansive form of Buddhism. It spread across regions such as China, Korea, Japan, and Vietnam. Mahayana texts expand upon and reinterpret the original teachings of the Buddha, emphasizing compassion and the bodhisattva ideal—a commitment to attaining enlightenment for the benefit of all sentient beings.

One of Mahayana's defining features is its emphasis on the notion of "emptiness" (shunyata), which challenges fixed notions of self and reality. Mahayana texts, such as the Mahayana Sutras, include the Lotus Sutra and the Heart Sutra, which explore the profound interconnectedness of everything. Mahayana allows individuals to engage with Buddhist principles within their daily lives.

Vajrayana Buddhism: The Diamond Vehicle

Vajrayana, often referred to as the "Diamond Vehicle," is a unique form of Buddhism that emerged in Tibet and the Himalayan region. It incorporates elements from Indian Tantra and indigenous traditions. Vajrayana places a strong emphasis on esoteric practices, including rituals, mantras, and meditation techniques, which are believed to expedite the path to enlightenment.

Vajrayana practitioners often receive empowerments and transmissions from qualified teachers, engaging in practices that are intended to transform ordinary experiences into profound insights. Tantra, a key component of Vajrayana, offers methods for harnessing the energies of the body, speech, and mind to accelerate spiritual growth. The visualization of deities and the use of sacred symbols are also prominent features of Vajrayana practice.

Diversity within Unity

Theravada, Mahayana, and Vajrayana Buddhism are distinct expressions of the teachings of the Buddha. While they vary in practices, philosophies, and cultural adaptations, these branches all share the common goal of attaining enlightenment and alleviating suffering.

Meditation and Mindfulness Practices: Inner Pathways to Peace and Clarity

Meditation and mindfulness are ancient practices that have transcended cultural and religious boundaries to become integral aspects of contemporary well-being. Rooted in traditions such as Buddhism, Hinduism, and Taoism, these practices offer profound tools for cultivating awareness, managing stress, and fostering a deeper connection to the present moment.

Meditation: The Journey Inward

Meditation is a practice that involves directing your attention inward to achieve a heightened state of mental clarity and inner peace. It encompasses a wide range of techniques, each with its own focus and purpose. Some common meditation practices include:

1. **Mindfulness Meditation**: This practice involves observing thoughts, sensations, and emotions without judgment. It cultivates awareness of the present moment, allowing you to develop a non-reactive and accepting stance toward life's experiences.

2. **Concentration Meditation**: Concentration techniques involve focusing on a single point of focus, such as the breath, a mantra, or a visual object. This practice enhances concentration and stillness of the mind.

3. **Loving-kindness Meditation (Metta)**: Metta meditation is centered around cultivating feelings of compassion and love, first for yourself and then extending those feelings to others, including loved ones, acquaintances, and even those with whom you may have difficulties.

4. **Transcendental Meditation**: This technique involves repeating a specific mantra to achieve a state of deep relaxation and expanded awareness.

5. **Vipassana Meditation**: Derived from Buddhist tradition, Vipassana meditation involves a detailed observation of bodily sensations and mental processes. It is aimed at gaining insight into the impermanent and interconnected nature of reality.

Mindfulness: Present-Centered Awareness

Mindfulness is the practice of paying deliberate and non-judgmental attention to the present moment. It involves observing thoughts, sensations, and emotions as they arise without becoming entangled in them. Mindfulness encourages you to accept experiences as they are, fostering a sense of detachment.

Jon Kabat-Zinn, a pioneer in bringing mindfulness to the West, describes mindfulness as "the awareness that arises through paying attention, on purpose, in the present moment, non-judgmentally."

This practice has gained significant recognition in the fields of psychology, medicine, and education due to its positive effects on stress reduction, emotional regulation, and overall well-being.

Benefits and Modern Applications

Both meditation and mindfulness practices offer many benefits:

1. **Stress Reduction**: Regular practice has been shown to reduce stress, anxiety, and even symptoms of depression.
2. **Cognitive Enhancement**: Meditation can improve focus, attention, and cognitive flexibility.
3. **Emotional Regulation**: Mindfulness can help you manage your emotions and respond to situations with greater clarity and calmness.
4. **Physical Health**: Meditation has been linked to reduced blood pressure, improved immune function, and enhanced overall physical health.

In recent years, mindfulness-based interventions have been integrated into therapies, schools, workplaces, and even prisons to promote well-being and resilience.

The Spread and Impact of Buddhism on Asia and Beyond

Buddhism's journey from its humble origins in ancient India to a global spiritual phenomenon is a testament to its enduring appeal and profound impact on cultures, societies, and individuals. As it spread across Asia and beyond, Buddhism adapted and transformed, resulting in a rich tapestry of traditions, practices, and beliefs that continue to shape the world today.

Spread of Buddhism: The Silk Road and Beyond

The trade routes of the Silk Road, connecting India with Central Asia, China, and eventually even reaching Southeast Asia, Korea, Japan, and Tibet, helped Buddhism spread across the region. As Buddhist monks and merchants traveled these routes, they carried not only goods but also the teachings and scriptures of Buddhism.

In Central Asia, Buddhism found fertile ground, leading to the establishment of vibrant Buddhist communities and the creation of magnificent art and architecture. In China, Buddhism blended with indigenous philosophies, resulting in the emergence of unique schools such as Chan (Zen in Japan), which emphasized direct insight and meditation. In Korea and Japan, Buddhism took root and intertwined with local customs, producing distinct cultural expressions of the religion.

Impact on Asian Societies: Culture, Art, and Philosophy

The spread of Buddhism brought about transformative changes in various Asian societies. Buddhist monasteries became centers of learning, preserving, and transmitting knowledge in an era before widespread literacy. Art and architecture flourished, as seen in the exquisite sculptures, paintings, and architectural marvels that adorned temples across the continent.

Buddhism's influence extended beyond religious realms, shaping philosophies and ethical systems. The emphasis on compassion, mindfulness, and the interconnectedness of all life left an indelible mark on Asian philosophies and values. Buddhist teachings influenced literature, ethics, governance, and the social fabric of societies.

Beyond Asia: Buddhism's Global Impact

The impact of Buddhism reached beyond the Asian continent, influencing Western thought in the modern era. As trade, exploration, and cross-cultural exchange expanded, Western scholars encountered

Buddhist ideas and texts. Translations and interpretations of Buddhist scriptures played a role in shaping European philosophical and spiritual discourse, particularly during the 19th and 20th centuries.

In recent decades, the popularity of mindfulness meditation and Buddhist concepts such as compassion and interconnectedness have gained global attention, influencing psychology, neuroscience, and wellness practices. The mindfulness movement, rooted in Buddhist principles, has found a place in therapeutic interventions, stress reduction programs, and corporate wellness initiatives.

A Living Legacy

The journey of Buddhism from India to Asia and beyond underscores its ability to adapt, integrate, and inspire diverse societies while offering insights into the nature of human existence, suffering, and the pursuit of enlightenment. The global legacy of Buddhism continues to remind humanity of its shared values and aspirations, inviting individuals of all backgrounds to explore the paths of compassion, wisdom, and inner transformation.

Chapter 3

Christianity

From the humble beginnings of a carpenter's son in Bethlehem to the spread of its message across continents and epochs, Christianity has woven threads of hope, salvation, and divine love into the very fabric of human experience. At its core lies the figure of Jesus Christ, whose life, teachings, and sacrifice have ignited hearts and ignited intellectual exploration for generations.

Through its triumphs and tribulations, Christianity remains an enduring testament to the boundless potential of faith to shape lives and illuminate the path towards transcendence.

The Life and Teachings of Jesus Christ: A Message of Love, Compassion, and Redemption

The life and teachings of Jesus Christ have left a permanent mark on human history, shaping cultures, societies, and the spiritual landscape of the world. As the central figure of Christianity, Jesus is revered not only for his role as the Messiah but also for his profound teachings that continue to resonate with millions across the globe.

Jesus of Nazareth, believed to have been born around 4 to 6 BCE in Bethlehem, Judea (modern-day Israel), grew up in a humble family in the town of Nazareth. Little is known about his early years, but the Gospels of the New Testament offer glimpses of his upbringing and his emergence as a spiritual teacher and healer.

At around age 30, Jesus embarked on a journey of preaching, healing, and transformative teachings. His central message focused on love, compassion, forgiveness, and the imminent arrival of the Kingdom of God—a spiritual realm characterized by justice, mercy, and harmony. Some of his core teachings include:

1. **The Sermon on the Mount**: Found in the Gospel of Matthew, where Jesus outlined the Beatitudes, a set of blessings for those who exemplified qualities like humility, meekness, and a hunger for righteousness.

2. **The Parables**: Jesus frequently used parables—simple stories with moral or spiritual lessons—to illustrate deeper truths. Parables like the Good Samaritan and the Prodigal Son conveyed messages of compassion, mercy, and the boundless love of God.

3. **The Greatest Commandments**: Jesus encapsulated his teachings in two commandments: to love God with all your heart, soul, and mind, and to love your neighbor as yourself. These principles emphasize the interconnectedness of love, faith, and ethical living.

4. **Forgiveness and Redemption**: Jesus emphasized the importance of forgiveness and redemption, teaching that anyone can find salvation through faith, repentance, and a willingness to turn away from negative acts.

Jesus' work was marked by his miraculous healings, which were not only physical but also symbolic of his capacity to heal spiritual wounds. He restored sight to the blind, cured the sick, and even raised the dead. These miracles served as demonstrations of his divine authority and compassion for human suffering.

The Crucifixion and Resurrection

The culmination of Jesus' life is his crucifixion, a pivotal event in Christian theology. According to the Gospels, Jesus was arrested, tried, and crucified under the orders of Roman authorities. Christians believe that through his sacrificial death, Jesus atoned for the sins of humanity, offering redemption and eternal life to those who believe in him.

The resurrection of Jesus, three days after his crucifixion, is celebrated as Easter—the event that symbolizes victory over death and the promise of eternal life. The resurrection serves as a cornerstone of Christian faith, embodying the hope and renewal that Christ's teachings offer.

Jesus' teachings have been interpreted and embraced by diverse cultures and denominations, leading to a spectrum of beliefs and practices within Christianity. From the early apostolic communities to the global church today, Jesus' message of salvation, grace, and the potential for spiritual transformation remains a beacon of hope for millions seeking meaning, purpose, and connection to the divine.

Central Beliefs in Christianity: Trinity, Salvation, and Afterlife

Christianity, with its diverse traditions and interpretations, is united by a core set of beliefs that provide a foundation for the faith's theology, ethics, and worldview. Among these central beliefs are the concepts of the Trinity, salvation, and the afterlife, which offer insights into the nature of God, the purpose of human existence, and the ultimate destiny of the soul.

The Trinity: One God in Three Persons

At the heart of Christian theology is the concept of the Trinity—the belief that God exists as three distinct but inseparable persons: God the Father, God the Son (Jesus Christ), and God the Holy Spirit.

While the term "Trinity" doesn't appear explicitly in the Bible, it is inferred from passages that depict the Father, Son, and Holy Spirit in relation to one another. The Trinity represents a mystery that has inspired theological contemplation for centuries, reflecting the intricate interplay between unity and diversity.

Salvation: Redemption and Grace

Salvation is a central theme in Christianity, representing the reconciliation of humanity with God through the redemptive work of Jesus Christ. The belief in salvation is rooted in the idea that human beings are inherently sinful and separated from God. Jesus' sacrificial death on the cross is seen as the means by which humanity's sins are forgiven and a restored relationship with God is made possible.

Christians believe that salvation is a gift from God, received through faith in Jesus Christ as Lord and Savior. This belief in Jesus' role as the redeemer underscores the transformative power of faith and the potential for spiritual rebirth.

Afterlife: Eternal Destiny

Christianity teaches that human existence extends beyond this earthly life. The concept of the afterlife is centered around the belief that each individual's soul will continue to exist after death, facing a judgment that determines its eternal destiny. Two primary destinations are identified:

1. **Heaven**: Often depicted as a realm of eternal communion with God, heaven is a place of ultimate happiness, fulfillment, and perfection. It is characterized by the absence of suffering, sin, and separation from God.

2. **Hell**: Hell is often portrayed as a state of eternal separation from God, characterized by suffering and spiritual anguish. While interpretations of hell vary, it is generally understood as a consequence of rejecting God's grace and refusing to align with divine love and goodness.

The specifics of the afterlife, including the nature of heaven and hell, vary among Christian denominations and perspectives. Some Christians believe in concepts like purgatory—a state of purification for souls destined for heaven but not yet fully cleansed from sin.

Foundations of Faith

The Trinity, salvation, and the afterlife form the bedrock of Christianity, encompassing the divine nature, the redemption of humanity, and the eternal destiny of souls. These central beliefs provide a lens through which Christians understand their relationship with God, the purpose of their lives, and the hope of eternal communion with the divine. Despite the variations in Christian interpretation, these core concepts continue to inspire devotion, reflection, and a sense of meaning in the lives of believers around the world.

Denominations within Christianity: Catholicism, Protestantism, and Orthodoxy

Christianity, as a diverse and widespread faith, has given rise to various denominations, each with distinct theological beliefs, practices, and traditions. Among the most significant branches are Catholicism, Protestantism, and Orthodoxy. These denominations embody different interpretations of scripture, church governance, and spiritual practices.

Catholicism: Ancient Tradition and Papal Authority

Central to Catholic theology is the belief in the primacy of the Bishop of Rome, the Pope, as the supreme spiritual authority. The Pope's teachings on faith and morals are considered infallible under specific conditions.

The Catholic Church places a strong emphasis on worship, sacraments, and the intercession of saints. The seven sacraments, including baptism, Eucharist, and confession, are considered conduits of divine grace. The veneration of Mary, the Mother of Jesus, and the saints is an integral aspect of Catholic piety.

Protestantism: Reformation and Personal Relationship

Protestantism emerged as a result of the Reformation in the 16th century, led by figures such as Martin Luther, John Calvin, and Ulrich Zwingli. Protestants emphasized the authority of scripture and the doctrine of salvation by faith alone (sola fide) rather than reliance on works. This marked a departure from Catholic teachings on justification.

Protestant denominations, which include Lutheranism, Calvinism, Anglicanism, and various evangelical groups, emphasize the individual's direct relationship with God. Worship styles vary, but many Protestants prioritize scripture reading, preaching, and congregational singing. The priesthood of all believers, the idea that all believers have direct access to God, is a hallmark of Protestant theology.

Orthodoxy: Ancient Traditions and Mystical Piety

Orthodoxy, also known as Eastern Orthodoxy or the Eastern Orthodox Church, traces its origins to the early Christian communities of the Eastern Mediterranean. It places a strong emphasis on preserving apostolic tradition, liturgical worship, and mystical spirituality. Unlike the Pope in Catholicism, the Orthodox Church is characterized by a conciliar model of governance, with collective decision-making by bishops.

Orthodox theology emphasizes theosis, the belief that humans can partake in the divine nature through a process of spiritual transformation. Iconography, elaborate liturgies, and the veneration of saints are distinctive features of Orthodox worship. The Divine Liturgy, a central liturgical service, reflects the continuity of ancient traditions.

Interplay and Diversity

Despite their distinct characteristics, these denominations share commonalities in their adherence to the Nicene Creed—a statement of faith that underscores the belief in the triune God. The Holy Scriptures, especially the New Testament, are foundational for all three branches.

While these denominations have historical differences and theological distinctions, there is also a rich dialogue and interaction among them.

Sacraments and Rituals in Christianity: Symbols of Spiritual Transformation

Sacraments and rituals hold a profound place within Christianity, serving as symbolic acts that connect believers to the divine and convey spiritual truths. These sacred practices, carried out across various denominations, are believed to impart God's grace, foster spiritual growth, and deepen a person's relationship with the divine.

Baptism: Initiation and Cleansing

Baptism is a foundational sacrament that signifies the initiation of a person into the Christian community. It is often considered a rite of passage, symbolizing the individual's rebirth and entry into the family of believers. Through the act of immersion or pouring of water, baptism represents the washing away of sin and the emergence of a new life in Christ.

In some Christian traditions, infant baptism is practiced, while others emphasize adult baptism as a conscious choice. Regardless of the method, baptism carries the message of spiritual cleansing, commitment to Christ, and unity with the larger Body of Christ.

Eucharist (Holy Communion): Nourishment of the Soul

The Eucharist, also known as Holy Communion or the Lord's Supper, holds central importance in Christian worship. This sacrament commemorates the Last Supper of Jesus with his disciples, where he shared bread and wine as symbols of his body and blood. The Eucharist emphasizes the sacrificial nature of Christ's death and the ongoing spiritual nourishment he offers to believers.

Bread and wine are consecrated through prayer, and Christians partake in the elements as a means of receiving Christ's presence. This act is understood to foster a deeper union with Christ and with fellow believers. Different Christian traditions interpret the Eucharist in various ways, ranging from a symbolic memorial to a belief in the real presence of Christ in the elements.

Confirmation: Empowerment and the Holy Spirit

Confirmation, often associated with the Roman Catholic, Eastern Orthodox, and Anglican traditions, is a sacrament that signifies the strengthening of a person's faith and the bestowal of the Holy Spirit. Usually performed after baptism, confirmation involves the laying on of hands by a bishop or priest and the anointing with chrism, a consecrated oil.

Confirmation is believed to equip the believer with the gifts of the Holy Spirit, enabling them to live out their faith courageously and make a public commitment to Christ. This sacrament underscores the continuity of a person's spiritual journey and their integration into the life of the Church.

Rites of Passage: Marriage and Anointing of the Sick

Marriage and the Anointing of the Sick, also known as Last Rites or Extreme Unction, are considered sacraments by many Christian traditions.

Marriage is celebrated as a sacred covenant between two individuals, reflecting the relationship between Christ and the Church. The ceremony varies among denominations but generally involves vows, blessings, and the exchange of rings. The sanctity of marriage is upheld as a representation of Christ's love for humanity.

The Anointing of the Sick is administered to those who are seriously ill or facing the end of life. This sacrament offers spiritual comfort and healing, emphasizing God's presence in times of suffering. It is often accompanied by prayers for physical and spiritual well-being.

Historical and Cultural Significance of Christianity: Shaping Civilizations and Worldview

Christianity's historical and cultural significance is deeply woven into the fabric of human civilization, leaving an impact on societies, art, governance, ethics, and the global worldview. From its origins in the ancient Near East to its spread across continents and centuries, Christianity's influence is vast and diverse, shaping the course of history and the way people perceive the world.

Foundations and Early Expansion

Christianity emerged in the Roman Empire, a vast multicultural and multireligious domain. The message of Jesus Christ, emphasizing love, compassion, and the Kingdom of God, resonated with individuals from various walks of life. Despite persecution, early Christian communities spread throughout the Roman world.

The conversion of Emperor Constantine in the 4th century marked a pivotal moment, as Christianity gained official recognition and support. The establishment of Constantinople (modern-day Istanbul) as the Eastern Roman Empire's capital further solidified the faith's influence.

Cultural Synthesis and Artistic Expression

Christianity's expansion and interaction with various cultures led to a rich synthesis of artistic styles, religious practices, and philosophical ideas. Iconography, illuminated manuscripts, and architecture became vehicles for expressing faith and reflecting theological concepts. Majestic cathedrals, such as Notre-Dame in Paris and St. Peter's Basilica in Vatican City, stand as testaments to Christianity's influence on architecture.

Christian art has depicted biblical narratives, saints, and theological themes, contributing to the visual language of Western civilization. The Renaissance, with its focus on humanism and the revival of classical learning, was deeply influenced by Christian thought and themes, resulting in masterpieces by artists like Michelangelo, Leonardo da Vinci, and Raphael.

Ethics, Governance, and Social Change

Christianity's ethical teachings, centered on love, justice, and the dignity of every human being as a creation of God, have influenced moral philosophies and societal norms. The development of just war theory, concepts of human rights, and the abolition of slavery were guided by Christian principles.

The Church's role in medieval Europe extended beyond the spiritual realm, as it wielded significant political and social power. Monasteries preserved knowledge, education, and medical care, while the spread of Christianity was often accompanied by efforts to improve living conditions and promote cultural exchange.

Global Expansion and Cultural Diversity

Christianity's spread beyond Europe during the Age of Exploration led to its interaction with diverse cultures in Africa, Asia, and the Americas. Missionaries and explorers introduced Christianity, sometimes resulting in cultural assimilation, syncretism, or the emergence of new forms of worship.

Christianity played a role in the development of modern nation-states, influencing legal systems, education, and governance structures. It also fostered the growth of academic institutions, where theology, philosophy, and science intersected.

Chapter 4

Islam

Islam stands as a guiding light that has illuminated hearts and minds for centuries. Rooted in the deserts of Arabia and borne on the wings of revelation, Islam's message of submission to the one true God has traversed continents, cultures, and epochs, leaving an indelible imprint on the world.

From the teachings of Prophet Muhammad to the resonance of the Quranic verses, Islam offers a path to transcendence, ethical clarity, and a deep connection with the divine.

Prophet Muhammad and the Quran: Foundations of Islam's Spiritual and Ethical Framework

The life of Prophet Muhammad and the revelations of the Quran form the cornerstone of Islam, a faith that emerged in the 7th century CE in the Arabian Peninsula. These foundational elements have profoundly shaped the beliefs, practices, and cultural expressions of over a billion Muslims worldwide.

Prophet Muhammad: The Messenger of God

Prophet Muhammad, born in Mecca around 570 CE, belonged to the tribe of Quraysh. He experienced a life marked by introspection and a deep spiritual yearning, often retreating to the cave of Hira for solitude and contemplation. At the age of 40, while meditating in the cave, Muhammad received his first revelation from the angel Gabriel. This event marked the beginning of his prophetic mission.

Muhammad's message centered on the worship of the one true God, known as Allah in Arabic. He emphasized the importance of compassion, social justice, and the ethical treatment of others. His teachings challenged the polytheistic beliefs prevalent in Mecca, advocating for a return to the monotheistic faith of Abraham.

The Quran: Revelation and Guidance

The revelations Muhammad received over the course of 23 years were compiled into the Quran, the holy scripture of Islam. Muslims believe that the Quran is the direct word of God, conveyed through the angel Gabriel to Muhammad. The Quran addresses a wide range of subjects, including theology, morality, law, and guidance for personal conduct.

Ethical Framework and Social Justice

Prophet Muhammad's life exemplified the ethical values written in the Quran. His treatment of orphans, widows, the poor, and the marginalized reflected a commitment to social justice and compassion. His teachings stressed the importance of honesty, integrity, and fairness in personal and communal dealings.

The Quran's call to establish a just and compassionate society has influenced Islamic jurisprudence and governance systems. Concepts such as Zakat (charitable giving), Sadaqah (voluntary charity), and the prohibition of usury aim to ensure the equitable distribution of resources and the alleviation of poverty.

Islamic Practices and Spirituality

The Five Pillars of Islam—Shahada (faith declaration), Salat (prayer), Zakat (giving to charity), Sawm (fasting during Ramadan), and Hajj (pilgrimage to Mecca)—serve as a practical framework for Muslims. These practices cultivate spiritual growth, communal solidarity, and ethical conduct.

Interfaith Dialogues and Cultural Impact

Prophet Muhammad's teachings and the Quran have fostered interfaith dialogues and influenced diverse cultural expressions. Islamic art, architecture, calligraphy, and literature have flourished, reflecting a reverence for divine beauty and the Quranic message. Islamic scholars have contributed to fields such as astronomy, medicine, philosophy, and mathematics.

The Five Pillars of Islam: Cornerstones of Muslim Faith and Practice

The Five Pillars of Islam represent the foundational principles that guide the lives of Muslims, shaping their faith, ethics, and relationship with God and fellow human beings. These practices are considered essential obligations for every Muslim, uniting people around the world in a shared commitment to worship, compassion, and social responsibility.

1. Shahada (Faith Declaration)

The Shahada is the fundamental declaration of faith in Islam: "La ilaha illallah, Muhammadur rasulullah," meaning "There is no god but Allah, and Muhammad is the Messenger of Allah." This declaration signifies the belief in the monotheistic nature of God and the prophethood of Muhammad. The Shahada serves as the core affirmation of a Muslim's faith, emphasizing the oneness of God and the acceptance of Muhammad as the final prophet.

2. Salat (Prayer)

Salat, or ritual prayer, is a fundamental practice in Islam and serves as a means of direct communication with Allah. Muslims are required to pray five times a day, facing the Kaaba in Mecca, which is considered the holiest site in Islam. The daily prayers take place at specific times: pre-dawn (Fajr), midday (Dhuhr), afternoon (Asr), sunset (Maghrib), and evening (Isha).

Prayer involves specific physical postures and recitations of verses from the Quran. These rituals help Muslims maintain a regular connection with God, express gratitude, seek forgiveness, and find guidance in their daily lives.

3. Zakat (Charitable Giving)

Zakat is the practice of giving charitable donations to those in need, often calculated as a percentage of a person's wealth or income. It serves as a means of wealth redistribution and social justice, emphasizing the responsibility of the affluent to support the less fortunate. Zakat helps address poverty, provide for basic needs, and promotes a sense of community.

4. Sawm (Fasting during Ramadan)

Sawm refers to fasting during the month of Ramadan, the ninth month of the Islamic lunar calendar. Muslims abstain from eating, drinking, and other physical needs from dawn until sunset. Fasting serves as a spiritual practice that cultivates self-discipline, empathy for the hungry, and a heightened awareness of a person's dependence on God. The fast is broken each evening with a meal called iftar.

Fasting also serves as a time for increased devotion, reflection, and reading of the Quran. It is an opportunity for Muslims to seek forgiveness, engage in charitable acts, and strengthen their connection with Allah.

5. Hajj (Pilgrimage to Mecca)

Hajj is the pilgrimage to the holy city of Mecca in Saudi Arabia, which is an obligatory duty for Muslims who are physically and financially able to undertake the journey. Hajj occurs annually during the Islamic lunar month of Dhu al-Hijjah. It involves a series of rituals, including walking around the Kaaba, standing at the plains of Arafat, and throwing pebbles at pillars representing Satan.

Hajj serves as a unifying experience for Muslims from diverse backgrounds, symbolizing equality, humility, and unity. The pilgrimage reinforces the idea of a global Muslim community and connects believers with the historical legacy of Abraham and the monotheistic tradition.

Sunni and Shia Divisions: Understanding the Branches of Islam

The division between Sunni and Shia Muslims is one of the most significant and complex subjects in the history of Islam. While both branches share core beliefs and practices, their differences in theological interpretation, leadership, and historical narratives have given rise to distinct traditions and identities within the Islamic world.

Historical Context: The Origins of the Schism

The division between Sunni and Shia Muslims traces back to the early days of Islam, following the death of Prophet Muhammad in 632 CE. The primary point of contention centered on the question of succession: who should lead the Muslim community, known as the ummah, after the Prophet's passing.

Sunni Islam: The Way of the Majority

Sunni Islam emerged from the belief that leadership should be determined through the consensus (ijma) of the Muslim community. The first four caliphs, known as the Rashidun Caliphs—Abu Bakr, Umar, Uthman, and Ali—were recognized as rightful leaders by Sunnis. Sunni Islam emphasizes the authority of the Quran and the Hadith (recorded sayings and actions of the Prophet) as primary sources of guidance.

Sunni Muslims constitute the majority of the Muslim world and can be found in various countries across the Middle East, North Africa, South Asia, and beyond. While there are multiple schools of theological thought within Sunni Islam, they share a common emphasis on unity, community consensus, and adherence to the teachings of the Prophet.

Shia Islam: The Partisans of Ali

Shia Islam, on the other hand, emerged from the belief that leadership should remain within the family of the Prophet Muhammad, specifically through his cousin and son-in-law, Ali ibn Abi Talib. Shia Muslims believe that Ali and his descendants, known as Imams, hold spiritual and temporal authority, representing a divinely appointed lineage.

Shia Islam is characterized by a profound devotion to the Imams, particularly the Twelve Imams recognized by Twelver Shia, the largest branch of Shia Islam. The relationship between the

Imams and their followers is marked by the concept of Wilayah, or divine leadership. Shia communities celebrate various religious observances, such as Ashura, which commemorates the martyrdom of Imam Hussein, the grandson of the Prophet.

The Sunni-Shia divide also has regional and cultural dimensions. Sunnis are more widespread across the Muslim world, while Shia populations are concentrated in countries like Iran, Iraq, Bahrain, and parts of Lebanon and Yemen. These geographical concentrations have often intersected with political dynamics and have led to tensions, conflicts, and power struggles.

However, it is important to note that the Sunni-Shia division is not solely about theological differences; it also encompasses cultural, political, and historical factors. Despite these differences, both Sunni and Shia Muslims share fundamental beliefs, such as the belief in the oneness of God (Tawhid) and the prophethood of Muhammad. There are also efforts within the Muslim world to foster unity and bridge the gaps between these two major branches.

Influence of Islam on Art, Science, and Philosophy: A Legacy of Intellectual and Cultural Enlightenment

Islam's rich intellectual and cultural heritage has influenced the fields of art, science, and philosophy, contributing to the advancement of human knowledge and shaping the development of civilizations in a profound and lasting way.

Art: Blending Spirituality and Aesthetics

Islamic art is characterized by its intricate geometric patterns, arabesques, calligraphy, and a prohibition on representing living beings. These artistic traditions emerged from a desire to create visual beauty that also resonated with Islamic principles. The integration of sacred geometry and patterns reflects a spiritual connection with the divine order of creation.

The art of Islamic architecture is exemplified by iconic structures such as the Alhambra in Spain, the Blue Mosque in Turkey, and the Great Mosque of Cordoba in Spain. These buildings demonstrate a fusion of geometric precision, artistic elegance, and spiritual symbolism.

Science: Pioneering Discoveries and Enlightenment

During the Islamic Golden Age (8th to 13th centuries), Islamic scholars made groundbreaking contributions to various scientific disciplines. One of the most significant achievements was the preservation and translation of Greek, Roman, and Persian works into Arabic. This exchange of knowledge laid the foundation for advancements in fields such as astronomy, medicine, mathematics, and optics.

Scholars like Al-Razi (Rhazes), Ibn Sina (Avicenna), and Alhazen (Ibn al-Haytham) made pioneering contributions to medicine, mathematics, and optics, respectively. Their works were later translated into Latin and influenced European scholarship during the Renaissance.

Philosophy: Bridging Reason and Faith

Islamic philosophy emerged as an intellectual bridge between faith and reason, drawing on Greek philosophy, especially the works of Plato and Aristotle. Early Muslim philosophers like Al-Kindi, Al-Farabi, and Ibn Sina engaged in exploring metaphysics, ethics, and the relationship between the material and the spiritual realms.

Ibn Rushd (Averroes) played a significant role in translating and interpreting Aristotle's works. His emphasis on reason and rationality led to discussions about the compatibility of philosophy with Islamic theology. The works of these philosophers, especially

Ibn Rushd, had a profound impact on the development of Western philosophy.

Cultural Exchange and Transmission

The translation movement that took place in Baghdad, Cordoba, and Cairo facilitated the transmission of knowledge from ancient civilizations to the Islamic world and beyond. Islamic scholars translated and synthesized works from Greek, Persian, Indian, and Chinese traditions, enriching the intellectual landscape and fostering cross-cultural dialogue.

Continuing Legacy and Global Impact

The influence of Islamic art, science, and philosophy has transcended time and geography. Arabic numerals, including the concept of zero, were transmitted to the West and became fundamental to modern mathematics. The medical and pharmacological knowledge of Islamic scholars laid the groundwork for later medical advancements. The art of calligraphy continues to be celebrated, and Islamic architectural motifs have influenced designs in various cultures.

Human Achievement

The impact of Islam on art, science, and philosophy is a testament to the capacity of human creativity, intellect, and spirituality to intertwine and contribute to the betterment of humanity. The legacy of Islamic achievements in these fields continues to inspire scholars, artists, and thinkers worldwide, serving as a reminder of the potential for intellectual and cultural enlightenment to transcend boundaries and enrich the human experience.

Chapter 5

Judaism

In human history, few religions have woven a more resilient and profound narrative than Judaism. This ancient monotheistic religion, with roots stretching back over millennia, has not only shaped the identity of a people but has left a mark on the moral, cultural, and intellectual fabric of the world. At its heart lies a journey of faith, a covenant with a divine presence, and a commitment to uphold values.

From its beginnings in the ancient lands of the Middle East to its influence on global thought, Judaism stands as a testament to the enduring power of belief, tradition, and the unbreakable bond between a people and their God.

Judaism: Covenant with Abraham and the Significance of the Torah

Judaism is defined by its foundational beliefs, practices, and the stories that shape its identity. Two central aspects that have profoundly influenced Jewish thought, history, and culture, are the Covenant with Abraham and the significance of the Torah.

Covenant with Abraham: The Birth of a People

The Covenant with Abraham, as described in the Hebrew Bible, marks a pivotal moment in the history of Judaism. Abraham, a patriarch and prophet, is regarded as the forefather of the Jewish people. According to the Book of Genesis, God establishes a covenant with Abraham, promising him descendants as numerous as the stars, the land of Canaan as an inheritance, and a special relationship between his descendants and God.

This covenant is emblematic of the unique bond between the Jewish people and their deity. It serves as the foundation of the Jewish people's identity, emphasizing themes of faith, trust, and the fulfillment of divine promises. Abraham's willingness to obey God's command, even when it involves personal sacrifice, symbolizes the core value of obedience to God's will.

The Torah: Divine Revelation and Moral Guidance

The Torah, meaning "instruction" or "teaching," holds a central place in Judaism as the most sacred and foundational text. It encompasses the first five books of the Hebrew Bible: Genesis, Exodus, Leviticus, Numbers, and Deuteronomy. According to Jewish tradition, the Torah was revealed by God to Moses on Mount Sinai.

The Torah is not only a historical account of the Jewish people's origins but also a comprehensive guide to ethical living, moral values, and religious practices. It contains laws (mitzvot) that cover a wide range of topics, including rituals, social justice, dietary rules, and interpersonal relationships. The Ten Commandments, a subset of the Torah, encapsulate fundamental principles for ethical conduct and worship.

The Torah's interpretation has been a dynamic process throughout Jewish history. Jewish scholars, known as rabbis, have engaged in textual analysis, commentary, and interpretation to extract deeper meanings and applications from the text. The oral tradition, known as the Talmud, contains discussions, debates, and elaborations on the Torah's teachings, reflecting the richness of Jewish thought and ethical exploration.

The concepts of covenant and Torah continue to shape Jewish thought and practice in the modern world. Jewish communities globally celebrate these foundational aspects through rituals, prayer, and study. The Covenant with Abraham reminds Jews of their shared heritage and responsibility to honor their covenant with God, while the study of the Torah provides a moral compass for navigating contemporary challenges.

Ten Commandments and the Moral Code in Judaism: A Blueprint for Ethical Living

At the heart of Judaism's ethical framework lies the Ten Commandments, a set of foundational principles that have guided Jewish thought and behavior for millennia. These commandments, revealed to Moses on Mount Sinai according to Jewish tradition, serve as a moral compass, offering a blueprint for ethical living and a harmonious relationship with both God and fellow human beings.

1. I am the Lord your God; you shall have no other gods before me.

This commandment establishes monotheism as the core of Jewish belief, emphasizing the exclusive worship of the one true God. It underscores the importance of spiritual devotion and loyalty to the divine.

2. You shall not make for yourself a graven image.

This commandment prohibits the creation of physical representations of God. It highlights the intangible nature of the divine and the potential pitfalls of idolatry, reminding believers to focus on the spiritual realm.

3. You shall not take the name of the Lord your God in vain.

Respect for God's name is central to this commandment. It encourages reverence in speech and thought, cautioning against using the divine name casually or frivolously.

4. Remember the Sabbath day and keep it holy.

Observing the Sabbath as a day of rest and spiritual rejuvenation is emphasized in this commandment. It reinforces the importance of setting aside time for worship, reflection, and familial connections.

5. Honor your father and mother.

This commandment underscores the significance of family relationships and respect for parents. It highlights the interconnectedness of generations and the values of honor and gratitude.

6. You shall not murder.

The sanctity of life is central to this commandment. It establishes the moral imperative to preserve and respect human life, discouraging violence and harm.

7. You shall not commit adultery.

This commandment promotes the values of fidelity and commitment in relationships. It emphasizes the importance of marital faithfulness and the bonds of trust.

8. You shall not steal.

This commandment upholds principles of honesty and property rights. It underscores the importance of respecting others' belongings and cultivating integrity.

9. You shall not bear false witness against your neighbor.

Truthfulness and honesty are emphasized in this commandment. It encourages the avoidance of lies and deceit, fostering trust and integrity in interactions.

10. You shall not covet.

This commandment cautions against the negative emotion of coveting, which can lead to envy and dissatisfaction. It encourages contentment and a focus on the blessings a person already has.

The Moral Code in Practice

The Ten Commandments serve as the foundation of Judaism's moral code, which extends beyond the individual to the community and society. The ethical teachings derived from these commandments encompass social justice, compassion, kindness, and responsibility. Jewish law, or Halakhah, further elaborates on how these principles translate into daily life and interactions.

Jewish Sects: An Exploration of Orthodox, Reform, and Conservative Traditions

Within Judaism, different sects have emerged over time, each offering distinct interpretations of beliefs, practices, and the role of tradition in contemporary life. Among the most notable Jewish sects are Orthodox, Reform, and Conservative Judaism. These diverse branches reflect a spectrum of approaches to religious observance, ritual, and engagement with the modern world.

Orthodox Judaism: Embracing Tradition and Law

Orthodox Judaism places a strong emphasis on adherence to traditional beliefs, practices, and religious law, as expressed in the Torah and the Talmud. Orthodox communities uphold the authority of halakhah (Jewish law) and view it as binding on all aspects of life. They maintain a commitment to preserving ancient customs, observances, and a strict interpretation of kosher dietary laws.

Orthodox Jewish communities are often characterized by traditional prayer styles, gender-segregated worship spaces, and a focus on preserving cultural norms. While modern Orthodox Jews may engage with secular society, they often do so while maintaining a strong commitment to their religious identity.

Reform Judaism: Adapting Tradition to Modernity

Reform Judaism emerged as a response to the changing social and intellectual landscape of the 19th century. Reform Jews seek to reconcile traditional values with modern thought, adapting religious practices to align with contemporary sensibilities. This branch emphasizes ethical teachings and principles, while often allowing greater flexibility in ritual observance.

Reform Jewish communities embrace inclusivity, gender equality, and progressive social values. Worship services may be conducted in both Hebrew and the group's native language, and there is an openness to reinterpretation of religious texts to reflect evolving contexts.

Conservative Judaism: Balancing Tradition and Change

Conservative Judaism occupies a middle ground between Orthodox and Reform approaches, aiming to strike a balance between tradition and modernity. Conservative Jews hold traditional beliefs and practices in high regard but are more willing to adapt certain aspects to contemporary life. They view halakhah as binding, but with room for interpretation.

Conservative Jewish communities often engage in innovative approaches to worship and education while maintaining a commitment to preserving key aspects of tradition. They value the study of Jewish texts and ethics, and they generally maintain more traditional prayer practices compared to Reform Judaism.

Despite their differences, Orthodox, Reform, and Conservative Judaism all share a common bond—their commitment to Judaism's rich heritage, teachings, and values. These diverse branches contribute to the vibrant and dynamic landscape of Jewish thought, allowing individuals and communities to express their spirituality and engage with their faith in ways that resonate with their unique perspectives and contexts.

The Synagogue: A Sacred Gathering Place

The synagogue stands as the spiritual heart of Jewish communities, serving as a place of worship, study, and communal connection. Derived from the Greek "synagoge," meaning "assembly," the synagogue represents more than just a physical structure; it also embodies the unity of the Jewish people in their devotion to God, Torah, and shared heritage.

Synagogues vary in architectural styles, reflecting the diverse cultures and regions in which they are found. The central sanctuary often houses the Ark, a cabinet containing the Torah scrolls, symbolizing the centrality of Torah in Jewish life. Bimah, a raised platform, is where the Torah is read, and congregants gather for prayer and study.

Beyond prayer services, synagogues host a multitude of activities, including Torah study sessions (Talmud Torah), cultural events, lifecycle ceremonies, and educational programs. The synagogue not only serves as a place for worship but also as a hub for community engagement, connecting individuals to their faith and to one another.

Shabbat: Embracing Rest and Reflection

Shabbat, the Jewish Sabbath, is a weekly day of rest, reflection, and renewal, observed from Friday evening at sundown to Saturday evening at nightfall. It is a cherished time for Jews to detach from the demands of daily life and focus on spirituality, family, and community.

Shabbat begins with the lighting of candles, ushering in a time of tranquility and connection with the divine. Blessings are recited over wine and bread (challah), symbolizing gratitude and sanctification. Throughout Shabbat, three prayer services—Friday evening, Saturday morning, and Saturday afternoon—take place in the synagogue, engaging participants in communal worship.

Shabbat encourages Jews to engage in restful and spiritually nourishing activities. Families gather for festive meals, engage in meaningful conversations, and immerse themselves in prayer, song, and study. Shabbat not only rejuvenates the soul but also reinforces the significance of communal bonds and the rhythm of life's sacred rhythms.

Passover: Celebrating Liberation and Renewal

Passover, or Pesach, is one of the most significant festivals in Judaism, commemorating the Exodus from Egypt and the Jews' liberation from slavery. The holiday is observed for seven days (eight in the Diaspora), during which Jews reflect on their history, celebrate freedom, and renew their commitment to faith.

The centerpiece of the Passover observance is the Seder, a festive meal full of symbolic foods, retelling of the Exodus story, and recitation of the Haggadah—the text that guides the Seder's proceedings. The unleavened bread (matzah) symbolizes the haste with which the Israelites left Egypt, and the bitter herbs evoke the bitterness of slavery.

Passover underscores the themes of redemption and gratitude. The holiday unites generations as families gather to share the Seder experience, connecting past and present while fostering a sense of continuity in the face of change.

Hanukkah: Kindling the Lights of Dedication

Hanukkah, the Festival of Lights, celebrates the triumph of light over darkness and the rededication of the Holy Temple in Jerusalem after its desecration. It is observed for eight days, beginning on the 25th day of the Hebrew month of Kislev, typically falling in December.

At the heart of Hanukkah is the lighting of the menorah, a nine-branched candelabrum. Each night, one additional candle is kindled, commemorating the miracle of the oil that burned for eight days instead of one. Families gather around the menorah, reciting blessings and engaging in festive songs and traditional foods, particularly those cooked in oil.

Hanukkah's significance extends beyond the miracle of the oil. It serves as a reminder of the enduring struggle for religious freedom and cultural identity. The holiday's themes of hope, resilience, and the power of light to dispel darkness resonate with Jews worldwide, fostering a sense of unity and celebration.

Historical Challenges and Contributions Shaping Judaism's Journey

Judaism's history is complex, full of challenges and contributions that shaped its evolution, resilience, and profound impact on the world. From trials that tested the faith to enduring legacies that have enriched humanity, Judaism's historical narrative is a testament to the enduring spirit of a people and their commitment to their beliefs.

Challenges: Sustaining Identity Through Struggles

1. **Exile and Diaspora:** The Jewish people faced numerous exiles and dispersions throughout history, starting with the Babylonian Exile and continuing through the Roman destruction of the Second Temple, the Spanish Inquisition, and beyond. These challenges forced Jews to adapt to new environments while striving to preserve their unique identity and religious practices.

2. **Persecution and Anti-Semitism:** From medieval Europe to the Holocaust, Jews have faced persecution, discrimination, and violence due to their religious beliefs. Pogroms, expulsions, and discriminatory laws have tested the resilience of Jewish communities, forcing them to navigate a history marked by trauma.

3. **Cultural and Religious Preservation:** Throughout centuries of diaspora, the challenge of preserving Jewish culture, language, and religious practices remained crucial. The Talmud, a compilation of Jewish law and teachings, played a significant role in maintaining a sense of continuity and shared heritage.

Contributions: Enriching Civilization and Thought

1. **Ethical Monotheism:** Judaism's belief in the one true God and its emphasis on ethical behavior laid the foundation for monotheistic religions that followed. The Ten Commandments and Jewish ethical teachings set a moral standard that has influenced the development of Western ethics.

2. **Textual Preservation and Interpretation:** The preservation of the Hebrew Bible and the Talmud through meticulous copying

and interpretation ensured the continuity of Jewish thought and teaching. Rabbinic scholarship and commentary enriched the understanding of religious texts and their application.

3. **Influence on Monotheism:** Judaism's emphasis on monotheism and ethical living has had a profound influence on Christianity and Islam. Both religions trace their roots to the Abrahamic covenant and share key ethical principles with Judaism.

4. **Cultural Contributions:** Jewish culture has produced notable contributions in literature, philosophy, science, and the arts. Thinkers like Maimonides and Spinoza made significant contributions to philosophy, while Jewish authors and artists have enriched global cultural heritage.

5. **Modern Social Movements:** The values of justice, equality, and social responsibility found in Jewish teachings have inspired various social justice movements. Jewish activists played pivotal roles in civil rights struggles and the fight against apartheid.

Enduring the Test of Time

Judaism's historical journey encapsulates the profound resilience of a people who have navigated challenges while contributing significantly to humanity's intellectual and cultural legacy. The Jewish experience underscores the importance of preserving heritage, adapting to changing circumstances, and fostering a sense of unity despite diverse backgrounds.

Through its challenges and contributions, Judaism has impacted human civilization, enriching the world with ethical values, cultural richness, and a commitment to a better future. The story of Judaism serves as an inspiration, reminding us of the strength that arises from faith, community, and an unwavering dedication to enduring principles.

Chapter 6

Sikhism

Born in the fertile lands of India's Punjab region, Sikhism is a faith that celebrates the oneness of God, the inherent worth of every individual, and a relentless pursuit of truth. With its distinctive teachings, history, and transformative philosophy, Sikhism beckons us to embark on a journey of spiritual discovery that transcends borders and generations.

Guru Nanak and the Founding Principles of Sikhism

The foundations of Sikhism are anchored in the profound teachings of Guru Nanak Dev Ji, the revered founder and first Guru of the Sikh faith. Born in 1469 in Talwandi, present-day Nankana Sahib in Pakistan, Guru Nanak's life and teachings laid the groundwork for a spiritual and socio-religious revolution that continues to inspire millions worldwide.

Guru Nanak's early life was marked by a deep sense of introspection and a thirst for spiritual truth. As a young man, he demonstrated a remarkable inclination toward contemplation and compassion. His travels took him far and wide, from the sacred Ganges to the distant realms of the Middle East, where he engaged in profound dialogues with scholars of various faiths. It was during these journeys that he experienced spiritual revelations that would form the bedrock of Sikhism's principles.

Oneness of God: Ik Onkar

At the heart of Guru Nanak's teachings is the concept of Ik Onkar, which translates to "One God." Rejecting the divisions propagated by caste and creed, Guru Nanak emphasized the universal truth of a singular, formless, and omnipresent deity. This concept revolutionized religious thought at the time, emphasizing a direct connection between humanity and the divine, transcending rituals and intermediaries.

Equality and Social Justice

Guru Nanak's teachings embedded a resolute commitment to social equality. He advocated for the eradication of caste-based discrimination, gender inequality, and socioeconomic disparities. The institution of the langar, a communal kitchen offering free meals to all, irrespective of their background, was a manifestation of Guru Nanak's vision of equality and the rejection of societal hierarchies.

Three Pillars of Sikhism

Guru Nanak established the foundation of Sikhism on three key pillars:

1. **Naam Japna (Meditation on God's Name):** The practice of constant remembrance of God's name, coupled with contemplative meditation, fosters spiritual growth and connection.

2. **Kirat Karni (Earning a Living through Honesty):** Guru Nanak emphasized the importance of honest labor, emphasizing the dignity of work and the pursuit of livelihood through ethical means.

3. **Vand Chakna (Sharing with Others):** Sharing with those in need, selfless service, and contributing to the welfare of society are fundamental aspects of Sikhism's ethos.

Humility and Community Engagement

Guru Nanak's humility and devotion to service set an example for his followers. He believed in engaging with the world while remaining detached from its material entanglements. His teachings promoted selflessness, compassion, and a commitment to uplifting the marginalized or oppressed.

Legacy and Continuation

Guru Nanak's profound legacy extended beyond his own time. He established a community of followers who came to be known as Sikhs, who continued his teachings through subsequent Gurus. These teachings, compiled in the Guru Granth Sahib, the holy scripture of Sikhism, serve as a timeless guide for living a life of virtue, devotion, and service.

The founding principles of Sikhism, as espoused by Guru Nanak, remain as relevant today as they were during his lifetime. His teachings challenge societal norms, champion equality, and invite humanity to cultivate a deeper connection with the divine.

Belief in One God and the Principle of Equality in Sikhism

At the core of Sikhism lies a profound belief in the oneness of God and an unwavering commitment to the principle of equality. These foundational tenets, championed by Guru Nanak and carried forth by successive Sikh Gurus, form the spiritual bedrock upon which Sikhism stands. They shape not only the theology but also the social and ethical dimensions of this vibrant faith.

Belief in One God (Ek Onkar): Unity Amidst Diversity

Central to Sikhism is the concept of "Ek Onkar," which encapsulates the belief in the absolute oneness of God. This principle transcends the confines of any religious, cultural, or geographical boundaries, emphasizing the universality of the divine. Sikhism asserts that there is only one Creator, referred to as "Waheguru" or "Satnam," who is formless, eternal, and beyond human comprehension.

The belief in one God rejects polytheism, idol worship, and any division of the divine. It underlines the notion that all of humanity is interconnected and that diverse religious paths are simply different ways of approaching the same ultimate reality. This principle fosters religious harmony and encourages a sense of unity among all people.

Equality: A Foundational Pillar

Sikhism's commitment to equality is exemplified by its rejection of caste, class, and gender distinctions. Guru Nanak's teachings challenged the prevailing societal norms of his time, advocating for a radical reimagining of human relationships. This principle is enshrined in the Guru Granth Sahib, the holy scripture of Sikhism, which declares that all humans are equal in the eyes of God.

Equality Before God: Sikhism posits that all individuals, regardless of their background, have the potential to connect directly with the divine. There is no need for intermediaries, rituals, or priests. This concept of direct access to God underscores the intrinsic worth of every person and diminishes hierarchies within religious practice.

Egalitarian Worship: Sikhism practices communal worship in the Gurdwara, the Sikh place of assembly. Within the Gurdwara, everyone sits on the same level, regardless of social or economic status. This approach fosters a sense of unity and reinforces the belief in the equality of all.

Rejecting Discrimination: Sikhism's commitment to equality is reflected in its rejection of discriminatory practices such as the caste system. Guru Nanak actively challenged the caste-based hierarchy prevalent in his society, asserting that merit and character were the true measures of a person's worth.

Langar: A Symbol of Equality: The institution of the langar, a communal kitchen where free meals are served to all, regardless of background, epitomizes Sikhism's principle of equality. By breaking bread together, Sikhs demonstrate their commitment to eradicating hunger, fostering community, and transcending societal divisions.

Sikhism's belief in one God and the principle of equality holds profound implications for contemporary society. It challenges the prevalence of discrimination, prejudice, and social hierarchies. In a world marked by diversity and division, these principles remind humanity of the inherent interconnectedness of all people and the imperative to treat each other with respect and dignity.

The Five Ks and the Khalsa Community: Symbols of Identity and Spirituality in Sikhism

Central to the Sikh faith is the concept of the Five Ks, a set of distinct articles of faith that hold profound spiritual and cultural significance. These symbols are not merely physical adornments but represent a deep commitment to Sikh values, identity, and principles. The Five Ks are intrinsically linked to the establishment of the

Khalsa community, a collective of initiated Sikhs who exemplify the highest ideals of the faith.

The Five Ks: Emblems of Devotion and Identity

1. **Kesh (Uncut Hair):** Sikhs are encouraged to maintain uncut hair as a symbol of naturalness and acceptance of God's creation. Hair is seen as a gift from the divine and is not to be altered. For many Sikhs, wearing turbans over uncut hair signifies a commitment to their faith and identity.

2. **Kara (Steel Bracelet):** The kara is a steel bracelet worn on the wrist, symbolizing the unity of God and the eternal nature of the divine. It serves as a reminder of a person's connection to the divine and the values of Sikhism.

3. **Kanga (Wooden Comb):** The kanga represents cleanliness and discipline. It signifies the need to keep the body, mind, and actions pure. The comb also serves as a reminder to comb through one's thoughts and actions, removing negative influences.

4. **Kachera (Cotton Undergarment):** The kachera signifies modesty and self-control. It is a reminder of the commitment to ethical behavior and the importance of restraining your desires.

5. **Kirpan (Sword):** The kirpan is a ceremonial sword that symbolizes courage, self-defense, and the protection of the oppressed. It is not intended for aggression but serves as a reminder of the responsibility to stand up against injustice.

Khalsa: The Pure Ones

The Khalsa, meaning "pure," is a community of initiated Sikhs who have voluntarily committed to upholding the highest spiritual and ethical ideals of Sikhism. The establishment of the Khalsa took place on the day of Vaisakhi in 1699, when Guru Gobind Singh, the tenth Guru of Sikhism, initiated the first five members of the Khalsa.

This event marked a pivotal moment in Sikh history, solidifying the faith's distinct identity and sense of unity.

To become a part of the Khalsa community, Sikhs undergo a ceremony known as Amrit Sanchar, where they receive Amrit, a sweetened water that has been stirred with a double-edged sword, symbolizing spiritual transformation. This process involves a commitment to the principles of Sikhism, including the Five Ks.

The Khalsa community is called to exemplify the virtues of righteousness, equality, and selflessness. Khalsa Sikhs are often referred to as Singh (Lion) for men and Kaur (Princess) for women, highlighting their spiritual equality.

The Khalsa community is deeply rooted in principles of selfless service (seva), social justice, and the protection of the oppressed. Khalsa Sikhs are encouraged to uphold the dignity and rights of all individuals, irrespective of their backgrounds.

Worship Practices and the Golden Temple: Spiritual Sanctity in Sikhism

Worship practices hold a profound place in Sikhism, serving as a means of connecting with the divine and nurturing the spiritual journey. At the heart of these practices is the iconic Golden Temple, known as Sri Harmandir Sahib, in Amritsar, India. This sacred space not only represents the epitome of Sikh worship but also stands as a symbol of inclusivity, devotion, and community.

Congregational Worship:

Sikhs gather for congregational worship in the Gurdwara, which means "gateway to the Guru." The focal point of a Gurdwara is the Guru Granth Sahib, the holy scripture of Sikhism, which is treated with reverence and respect. Regular recitation and singing of hymns from the Guru Granth Sahib form the foundation of Sikh worship.

Daily Practices:

Sikhs engage in daily practices to foster spiritual growth and mindfulness. Nitnem, a daily regimen of prayers and readings, begins in the early hours of the morning and includes recitations from the Guru Granth Sahib. These practices guide Sikhs in their daily lives, promoting a sense of gratitude, humility, and connection with the divine.

Sangat and Pangat:

The concepts of Sangat (spiritual community) and Pangat (communal meal) are integral to Sikh worship. Sangat emphasizes the importance of coming together as a community for collective worship, learning, and support. Pangat underscores equality and community by sharing a meal—often in the langar, the communal kitchen of a Gurdwara—with people of all backgrounds, regardless of social status.

Kirtan and Gurbani:

Kirtan, the devotional singing of hymns from the Guru Granth Sahib, is a central element of Sikh worship. Accompanied by musical instruments, kirtan evokes a sense of spiritual ecstasy and deepens the connection with the divine. Gurbani, the teachings found in the Guru Granth Sahib, resonates through kirtan, inspiring devotion and reflection.

The Golden Temple: Sanctuary of Spiritual Splendor:

The Golden Temple, situated in Amritsar, is a striking embodiment of Sikh worship and architectural brilliance. Its golden dome and white marble exterior shimmer in the sunlight, drawing millions of pilgrims and visitors each year. The temple complex is surrounded by the Amrit Sarovar, a holy pool believed to possess healing properties.

A Sanctified Space:

The Golden Temple is revered as the holiest shrine in Sikhism, housing the Guru Granth Sahib. Pilgrims from all walks of life, irrespective of faith or background, are welcomed to experience the spiritual sanctity of the temple. The practice of removing your shoes, covering your head, and washing your feet before entering the temple signifies respect and humility.

Langar: Nurturing the Soul and Body:

The Golden Temple is renowned not only for its spiritual significance but also for its tradition of the langar. Here, volunteers selflessly prepare and serve free meals to thousands of visitors every day. This practice of seva (selfless service) exemplifies Sikh values of equality, compassion, and community.

Promoting Social Justice: Sikhism's Enduring Commitment

Sikhism, beyond its spiritual dimensions, has consistently upheld a strong commitment to social justice and equality. Rooted in the teachings of Guru Nanak and embraced by subsequent Gurus, this commitment has manifested in various ways throughout Sikh history, resonating as a clarion call for change, compassion, and the betterment of society.

Guru Nanak's Vision of Equality:

Guru Nanak Dev Ji, the founder of Sikhism, laid the foundation for social justice by vehemently opposing inequality and discrimination. He challenged the oppressive caste system, emphasizing the inherent worth of all individuals regardless of their social status. Guru Nanak's teachings underscored the importance of treating every person with respect and dignity, transcending societal divisions.

Langar: An Emblem of Equality:

The institution of langar—the community kitchen that serves free meals to all, irrespective of background—is a striking embodiment of Sikhism's commitment to equality. Langar erases distinctions of caste, class, and gender, emphasizing the principle of oneness. Every Sikh Gurdwara across the world offers langar, inviting people to share in the experience of unity and service.

Social Activism and Advocacy:

Sikhs have historically engaged in social activism and advocacy to address issues of injustice. From the time of Guru Nanak to contemporary times, Sikh leaders and communities have raised their voices against oppression, inequality, and human rights violations. Sikhism's values of truth, compassion, and justice have propelled Sikhs to champion causes beyond their own community.

Standing Against Tyranny:

Sikh history is punctuated by instances of standing up against tyranny. The martyrdom of Guru Arjan Dev Ji and Guru Tegh Bahadur Ji, who sacrificed their lives for the right to practice their faith freely, symbolizes the broader fight against religious persecution and the defense of fundamental rights.

Sikh Role in Movements:

Sikhs have actively participated in various social justice movements worldwide. In the fight against racial discrimination and civil rights violations, Sikhs have stood alongside marginalized communities, including African Americans, advocating for equality and justice.

Championing Humanitarian Aid:

Sikh organizations have been at the forefront of humanitarian aid, responding to disasters and crises globally. The concept of "Sewa," or selfless service, drives Sikhs to provide relief and support to those in need, reflecting a commitment to alleviate suffering and promote social welfare.

Sikhism's unwavering commitment to social justice stands as a beacon of hope and inspiration. From Guru Nanak's visionary teachings to the modern-day efforts of Sikh individuals and organizations, the faith's principles have continually fueled endeavors to create a just and equitable world.

Sikhism's role in promoting social justice serves as a powerful reminder that spirituality and activism are not mutually exclusive, but rather intertwined in the pursuit of a more compassionate and equitable global community.

Chapter 7

Bahá'í Faith

In a world often marked by divisions, the Bahá'í Faith shines as a beacon of unity, equality, and spiritual illumination. Emerging from the heart of the 19th century, the Bahá'í Faith carries a profound message of harmony among all people and faiths.

With its emphasis on universal principles, social justice, and the essential oneness of humanity, the Bahá'í Faith invites us to embark on a journey of understanding, compassion, and the pursuit of a better world.

Life of Bahá'u'lláh and His Transformative Teachings

The life of Bahá'u'lláh, the founder of the Bahá'í Faith, is a testament to resilience, spiritual insight, and the profound impact that a single individual can have on the course of history. Born in 1817 in Tehran,

Persia (modern-day Iran), Bahá'u'lláh's life journey is characterized by a series of revelations, exiles, and teachings that have shaped the Bahá'í Faith into a global movement of unity and hope.

Early Life and Noble Heritage:

Bahá'u'lláh, originally named Mirza Husayn-Ali, hailed from a noble and respected family. From a young age, his intellect, compassion, and innate spirituality stood out. His early life was marked by his father's position at the Persian court, where Bahá'u'lláh gained exposure to the cultural, political, and social dynamics of his time.

In 1844, Bahá'u'lláh became a prominent figure within the Bábí movement, which was a precursor to the Bahá'í Faith. He later emerged as the central figure of the Bahá'í Faith, proclaiming his divine mission in 1863. He adopted the title "Bahá'u'lláh," meaning "Glory of God," signifying his role as the bearer of a new spiritual message for humanity.

Bahá'u'lláh's proclamation drew attention from religious and political authorities, leading to a series of exiles and imprisonments. He was banished from Persia to Baghdad, then to Istanbul, and eventually to the remote penal colony of Akka in Palestine (now Israel). Despite the harsh conditions, Bahá'u'lláh's teachings continued to flourish, and he received countless visitors seeking guidance and insight.

Key Teachings:

Bahá'u'lláh's teachings are transformative in their scope and impact:

1. **Unity of Religion and Humanity:** Bahá'u'lláh emphasized the essential unity of all religions, portraying them as progressive stages in the unfolding of a single spiritual truth. He envisioned a world where people of different faiths could unite in a common purpose.

2. **Oneness of God:** Bahá'u'lláh reiterated the belief in one God, emphasizing that all religions derive from the same divine source.

3. **Harmony of Science and Religion:** Bahá'u'lláh advocated for the harmony between science and religion, asserting that they are complementary avenues to uncovering truth.

4. **Universal Peace:** Bahá'u'lláh envisioned a future where nations would lay down their weapons and conflicts would give way to lasting peace. He proposed the establishment of a world federation to ensure global harmony and justice.

5. **Elimination of Prejudice:** Bahá'u'lláh condemned all forms of prejudice, whether based on race, religion, or nationality. His teachings promote the idea that all human beings are equal and deserving of respect.

6. **Gender Equality:** Bahá'u'lláh championed the equality of women and men, advocating for their equal rights and opportunities in all spheres of life.

Bahá'u'lláh's teachings have transcended borders and cultures, influencing millions of followers around the world. The Bahá'í Faith has become a unifying force that strives to build a more just, unified, and peaceful world. Bahá'u'lláh's legacy continues to inspire individuals, communities, and institutions to work towards social transformation and the realization of his vision for a harmonious global society.

Unity of Religion and Humanity: Bridging Spiritual Divides

At the heart of the Bahá'í Faith lies a profound concept that seeks to bridge the spiritual divides that have separated humanity throughout history: the unity of religion and humanity. This principle carries a transformative message that invites individuals and societies to recognize the essential oneness of all faiths and people.

The Oneness of Religion:

Bahá'u'lláh proclaimed that all the world's major religions emanate from the same divine source, representing different stages in the spiritual evolution of humanity. He envisioned these religions as interconnected chapters in a single unfolding narrative, each tailored to the needs of the time and culture in which it appeared.

Harmony Amid Diversity:

The Bahá'í teachings stress that the underlying spiritual truths found in various religions far outweigh their superficial differences. While religious practices and rituals may vary, the core principles of love, compassion, justice, and ethical behavior are universal, transcending cultural and doctrinal distinctions. This perspective fosters understanding and harmony among different faith communities.

Promoting Religious Tolerance:

The unity of religion and humanity challenges religious prejudice and intolerance. Bahá'ís believe that by acknowledging the divine origins of different faiths, individuals can approach discussions about religion with open hearts and minds, seeking common ground rather than perpetuating divisive arguments. This approach promotes religious tolerance and paves the way for interfaith dialogue.

Building Bridges Across Faiths:

The unity of religion and humanity encourages followers of all faiths to engage in constructive conversations about shared values, ethics, and aspirations. It encourages religious leaders to emphasize the fundamental principles of love, compassion, and unity that underpin their respective faiths, while demonstrating that the divisions created by dogma and ritual are often distractions from these core teachings.

Social Implications:

The principle of unity of religion and humanity extends beyond theological discussions. It has practical implications for addressing global challenges. By recognizing our shared spiritual heritage and common humanity, people are inspired to collaborate in addressing issues such as poverty, inequality, environmental degradation, and social injustice.

Challenges and Opportunities:

Implementing the unity of religion and humanity concept requires overcoming deeply ingrained prejudices and historical tensions. However, it offers a unique opportunity for healing and reconciliation. Embracing the principle can empower individuals to transcend divisive rhetoric, replace hostility with empathy, and contribute to the creation of a more inclusive and harmonious world.

A Path Toward Global Harmony:

The unity of religion and humanity encapsulates a vision where diverse faiths no longer serve as barriers but rather as bridges for understanding and cooperation. Bahá'u'lláh's teachings invite us to recognize that beneath many expressions of faith lies a shared human longing for connection to the divine and a commitment to moral and ethical principles.

By nurturing this unity, humanity can transcend differences, fostering a world where faith becomes a unifying force rather than a divisive one, and where the shared goal of human betterment takes precedence over doctrinal disagreements.

Principles of the Bahá'í Faith: Oneness, Equality, and Peace

The Bahá'í Faith, rooted in the teachings of Bahá'u'lláh, is built upon a foundation of profound principles that shape its spiritual ethos and guide the lives of its followers. Three fundamental principles stand as pillars of the Bahá'í Faith: oneness, equality, and peace.

These principles not only encapsulate the essence of the faith but also hold the potential to transform individuals and societies, fostering a world of unity and compassion.

Oneness:

The principle of oneness lies at the heart of the Bahá'í teachings, reflecting the belief in the essential unity of all things. Bahá'ís recognize that humanity, despite its diversity of cultures, races, and religions, is interconnected and part of a single human family. This recognition extends beyond the realm of humanity to encompass the entire creation, emphasizing a harmonious relationship between humans and the natural world. Bahá'ís view oneness as a spiritual truth that encourages empathy, cooperation, and a commitment to global well-being.

Equality:

The Bahá'í Faith places a strong emphasis on equality, rejecting all forms of prejudice, discrimination, and injustice. Bahá'u'lláh proclaimed the equality of all individuals, irrespective of their race, gender, social background, or nationality.

This principle is not confined to mere theoretical notions; it is a call to action, urging Bahá'ís to actively engage in efforts that promote social justice, uplift marginalized communities, and eradicate disparities in all spheres of life. The pursuit of equality aligns with the belief that every human being possesses inherent dignity and worth.

Peace:

Peace, both inner and global, is a central theme in Bahá'í teachings. Bahá'ís view peace as more than the absence of conflict; it is a dynamic state of harmony, understanding, and unity. The Bahá'í Faith advocates for the elimination of prejudices and the resolution of disputes through dialogue and consultation.

Beyond individual tranquility, Bahá'ís are encouraged to work toward the establishment of world peace through measures that address root causes of conflict, such as economic inequality and lack of education.

Interconnectedness of Principles:

These principles of oneness, equality, and peace are intricately interconnected. Oneness fosters a sense of kinship among all people, enabling the recognition of equality as a natural extension of shared humanity. This equality, in turn, lays the foundation for peaceful coexistence and the resolution of conflicts. Together, these principles weave a tapestry of spirituality, ethics, and social responsibility that guide Bahá'ís in their daily lives and interactions.

Application in Modern Context:

In an era marked by division, inequality, and strife, the principles of the Bahá'í Faith carry a timeless relevance. They offer a blueprint for transforming individuals and societies, encouraging people to transcend narrow boundaries and collaborate for the common good. These principles inspire Bahá'ís to actively contribute to the betterment of the world, whether through community-building activities, social initiatives, or engagement in interfaith dialogues.

Administrative Structure and Community Life in the Bahá'í Faith

The Bahá'í Faith, with its vision of unity and global transformation, has developed a unique administrative structure that fosters community cohesion, collective decision-making, and the pursuit of social progress. This structure, designed by Bahá'u'lláh and further developed by his son, `Abdu'l-Bahá, and subsequent leaders, is characterized by its decentralized nature, consultation-based decision-making, and emphasis on service to humanity.

Local Spiritual Assemblies:

At the grassroots level, Bahá'í communities are organized around Local Spiritual Assemblies. These assemblies, elected annually by adult Bahá'ís, are responsible for fostering spiritual growth, organizing community activities, and addressing the needs of individuals. They promote unity, ensure the welfare of their members, and serve as sources of guidance and support.

National Spiritual Assemblies:

Each country or territory with a significant Bahá'í presence has a National Spiritual Assembly, elected annually by delegates from Local Spiritual Assemblies. National Spiritual Assemblies guide the activities of the Bahá'í community within their jurisdiction, collaborate on regional and national initiatives, and represent the community to the broader society.

The Universal House of Justice:

At the international level, the highest governing body of the Bahá'í Faith is the Universal House of Justice. Elected every five years by National Spiritual Assemblies, this institution provides global leadership and guidance. It addresses issues of universal concern, interprets the Bahá'í teachings, and promotes the worldwide expansion of the faith.

Consultation: Heart of Decision-Making:

Consultation is a cornerstone of the Bahá'í administrative structure. Decision-making occurs through a process of collective consultation, where individuals contribute their insights, perspectives, and expertise. This process is characterized by a spirit of humility, openness, and a genuine search for truth. Consultation encourages unity, helps avoid divisive disputes, and ensures that decisions are informed by a diversity of viewpoints.

Community Life and Activities:

Bahá'í community life is characterized by activities that reflect the principles of the faith. Regular gatherings for prayer, devotional meetings, and study of sacred texts foster spiritual growth and community building. Service projects, ranging from literacy programs to environmental initiatives, are undertaken to contribute to the betterment of society.

Contributions to Society:

The Bahá'í administrative structure supports initiatives that promote social progress, such as education, healthcare, and poverty alleviation. Bahá'í-inspired schools, training programs, and development projects aim to empower individuals and communities to contribute positively to their societies.

Harmony of Spiritual and Material Aspects:

The Bahá'í administrative structure not only governs the community but also serves as a model of harmonizing spiritual principles with practical affairs. It exemplifies how a faith community can organize itself to create a better world while nurturing the spiritual growth of its members.

Emphasis on Global Harmony: A Cornerstone of the Bahá'í Faith

Emphasizing the intrinsic oneness of humanity, the Bahá'í teachings champion the ideals of unity, peace, and cooperation across cultures, nations, and religions. This emphasis on global harmony is not only a key principle of the Bahá'í Faith but also a call to action to build a world where the common bonds of humanity surpass divisions.

Unity in Diversity:

The Bahá'í Faith advocates for the harmonious coexistence of all races, cultures, and religions. It recognizes that diversity is a source of strength, enriching the human experience. The principle of unity in diversity challenges the artificial barriers that perpetuate conflict, intolerance, and inequality. Through fostering understanding and empathy, the Bahá'í teachings promote a sense of global citizenship that transcends national and cultural boundaries.

Elimination of Prejudice:

Prejudice and discrimination are identified as obstacles to global harmony. The Bahá'í Faith places great emphasis on eradicating prejudices of all forms, whether based on race, gender, religion, or nationality. The eradication of prejudice is not merely a personal endeavor but a collective one, requiring a transformation in attitudes and behaviors to create an environment where everyone is treated with dignity and respect.

The Power of Education:

Education plays a pivotal role in realizing global harmony. The Bahá'í teachings stress the importance of universal education that nurtures both the intellectual and spiritual faculties of individuals. Education is viewed as a means to empower individuals to contribute to their communities and societies, fostering a sense of responsibility for the well-being of all people.

Collaboration and Cooperation:

The Bahá'í Faith envisions a world where nations collaborate for the common good, transcending self-interest and prioritizing the welfare of all humanity. Cooperation among nations, driven by a shared commitment to justice and global progress, is seen as essential for achieving lasting peace and prosperity.

Religion as a Unifying Force:

The Bahá'í Faith perceives religion as a unifying force, capable of inspiring individuals and communities to transcend their differences. It teaches that the world's religions are interconnected and should be viewed as chapters in a single unfolding narrative. By recognizing the divine origins of all faiths, believers are encouraged to engage in meaningful interfaith dialogues that promote understanding and cooperation.

World Peace: A Collective Endeavor:

The Bahá'í teachings place great emphasis on the establishment of world peace. This is not merely the absence of conflict, but a state characterized by justice, security, and the flourishing of human potential. Achieving world peace requires collective efforts, including disarmament, the resolution of conflicts, and addressing the root causes of strife.

Emphasizing global harmony, the Bahá'í Faith presents a visionary and practical blueprint for a world that transcends the divisions that have plagued human history. By promoting unity, diversity, justice, and cooperation, the Bahá'í teachings offer a hopeful vision of a global community that works together to address challenges and uplift humanity as a whole.

The Bahá'í emphasis on global harmony extends an invitation to all individuals, regardless of their background, to participate in the co-creation of a more harmonious and unified world.

CHAPTER 8

Shinto

In the heartland of Japan's culture lies a spiritual tradition that is as ancient as the land itself—Shinto. Rooted in the harmonious relationship between humans, nature, and the divine, Shinto embodies the essence of Japan's soul and cultural identity.

From vibrant festivals that celebrate the changing seasons to the serene beauty of shrines nestled in natural landscapes, Shinto beckons us to embark on a journey of reverence, wonder, and connection to the mystical forces that shape both the physical and spiritual realms.

Nature-Based Spirituality in Japan: Harmony with the Divine Cosmos

This profound connection to the natural world finds its expression in Shinto, a traditional belief system deeply rooted in the Japanese psyche. Shaped by the awe-inspiring beauty of landscapes, the shifting seasons, and the forces of nature, this spirituality beckons us to embrace a harmonious coexistence with the cosmos.

In Shinto, nature is not just a backdrop—it is infused with the divine. The Japanese term "kami" encompasses a spectrum of divine entities, which can manifest as spirits inhabiting natural elements like trees, rocks, rivers, and mountains. This belief endows nature with a sacredness that is to be revered and protected, fostering a sense of responsibility toward the environment.

Shinto shrines are often nestled in serene natural settings, demonstrating the inseparable bond between the sacred and the natural. These shrines are gateways to the spiritual realm, serving as places of communion between humans and the kami. Torii gates, marking the entrance to sacred spaces, symbolize the threshold between the ordinary and the divine.

Seasonal Festivals:

The rhythm of nature's cycles is echoed in Shinto festivals that celebrate the changing seasons. Cherry blossom festivals, rice planting ceremonies, and autumn harvest rituals connect people to the ebb and flow of nature's energies. These celebrations reflect an understanding that human existence is intricately woven into the fabric of the natural world.

Purification Rituals:

Shinto places emphasis on purity and cleansing rituals that mirror the cleansing forces of nature. Rituals involve symbolic actions like washing the hands and mouth before entering a shrine, signifying a physical and spiritual purification. These practices reinforce the concept of living in harmony with both the physical and metaphysical realms.

Mountains as Sacred Space:

Mountains, often considered the dwelling places of kami, hold immense spiritual significance. Mount Fuji, Japan's iconic peak, is not only a symbol of beauty and power but also a revered pilgrimage site for spiritual seekers. Ascending a mountain is not only a physical journey but a spiritual one, reflecting the desire to commune with the divine.

The Philosophy of Animism:

Shinto's nature-based spirituality reflects an animistic philosophy—an understanding that everything in the natural world possesses a spirit. This perspective encourages mindfulness, respect, and an understanding of humanity's interconnectedness with all living things.

Preservation and Modernity:

As Japan modernizes, its commitment to nature-based spirituality remains steadfast. Efforts to protect sacred groves, pristine forests, and natural habitats reflect a deep-rooted reverence for the environment. Modern Shinto practitioners engage in efforts to conserve and preserve nature as an integral part of their spiritual practice.

Embracing Nature's Wisdom:

Nature-based spirituality in Japan extends an invitation to rekindle a connection that is often obscured in our urbanized and technology-driven world. It urges us to listen to the whispers of the wind, witness the unfolding of petals, and find solace in the rustling leaves.

Through Shinto's lens, we learn to tread lightly on the Earth, recognizing that our existence is intricately woven into the intricate tapestry of the natural world—an eternal dance of awe, respect, and symbiotic harmony.

Kami and Shrines in Shinto: Bridging the Human and Divine Realms

At the heart of Shinto lies a profound concept that infuses the natural world with the divine—the notion of "kami." These spiritual entities, often translated as gods or spirits, are revered as manifestations of the sacred within nature. The connection between kami and the tangible world is embodied in Shinto shrines, where people come to commune with the divine, seek blessings, and express their reverence for the natural order.

Kami are not singular deities with fixed forms or personalities. They can be found in the elements of nature—trees, rocks, rivers, and mountains—as well as in phenomena like wind, rain, and lightning. This animistic perspective extends the sacred to all aspects of creation, reflecting a belief in the interconnectedness of all existence.

Kami are perceived to possess both a tranquil and a fierce aspect. Some kami are associated with serenity and benevolence, while others exhibit a more powerful and even wrathful character. This dual nature underscores the complexity and diversity of forces at work in the universe, embodying the balance between creation and destruction.

Shrines as Sacred Spaces:

Shinto shrines serve as portals to the divine realm, where people can interact with kami and seek their blessings. These sacred spaces are meticulously designed to harmonize with the natural surroundings, reinforcing the inseparable bond between the spiritual and the natural. Torii gates, stone lanterns, and purification rituals all play a role in facilitating the connection between the human and the divine.

Worship at Shinto shrines often involves rituals that emphasize purity and respect. Visitors cleanse themselves before entering the shrine precincts, symbolizing both physical and spiritual purification. Offerings of food, sake, and symbolic items are made to honor and appease the kami. Clapping hands, ringing bells, and bowing further express reverence and gratitude.

Festivals and Seasonal Celebrations:

Shrines come alive during festivals, which are often rooted in the changing seasons and the cycles of nature. These celebrations highlight the dynamic relationship between kami and the natural world. Matsuri, or festivals, involve processions, performances, and communal activities that reflect Japan's cultural and spiritual heritage.

Shrines also cater to individual and collective devotion. While individuals seek personal guidance and blessings from kami, communities gather to celebrate shared values and traditions. This balance between personal spirituality and communal harmony is a hallmark of Shinto's influence on Japanese society.

Rituals and Festivals in Shinto: Hatsumode and Gion Matsuri

Rituals and festivals form the vibrant heart of Shinto. They not only connect individuals with the divine but also celebrate the rich tapestry of nature, culture, and community. Two significant examples are "Hatsumode," the New Year's shrine visit, and the "Gion Matsuri," one of Japan's most iconic festivals. These rituals and festivals exemplify the intricate interplay between spirituality, tradition, and collective identity in Japanese society.

Hatsumode: Welcoming the New Year with Renewed Spirituality

Hatsumode, literally meaning "first shrine visit," is a cherished tradition that marks the beginning of the New Year in Japan. It's a time for individuals and families to seek blessings, offer prayers, and express gratitude for the year past and the one ahead. Thousands flock to Shinto shrines across the country, creating a festive and contemplative atmosphere.

Ritual Components of Hatsumode:

1. **Purification:** Before approaching the shrine, visitors cleanse themselves with water to ensure physical and spiritual purity.

2. **Offerings:** People make monetary offerings, offer symbolic items, and write wishes on wooden plaques called "ema."

3. **Prayers:** In front of the main shrine hall, individuals bow, clap their hands, and offer their prayers to the kami, seeking blessings for health, success, and well-being.

4. **Omikuji:** Fortune-telling paper slips called "omikuji" are drawn, revealing predictions for the coming year. Positive fortunes are kept, while negative ones are tied to trees or racks to leave any bad luck behind.

Hatsumode is more than a religious ritual; it's a cultural practice that fosters a sense of renewal, hope, and community. It underscores the importance of starting the year on a spiritually positive note and encourages introspection and gratitude.

Gion Matsuri: A Festival of Tradition and Spectacle

The Gion Matsuri, celebrated in Kyoto during the month of July, is one of Japan's most famous festivals. Rooted in a tradition dating back over a millennium, Gion Matsuri celebrates the vibrant heritage of the city and pays homage to the kami for protection against natural disasters and epidemics.

Festival Highlights:

1. **Yamaboko Floats:** The festival is renowned for its elaborate floats, known as "yamaboko." These towering structures are adorned with intricate textiles, art, and craftsmanship.

2. **Processions:** The Gion Matsuri comprises two main processions: the "Saki Matsuri" and the "Ato Matsuri." During these processions, the yamaboko floats are paraded through the streets of Kyoto in a breathtaking display of tradition and community spirit.

3. **Religious Ceremonies:** While the festival is known for its grandeur, it also includes solemn religious ceremonies at Yasaka Shrine, the spiritual center of the festival.

4. **Cultural Performances:** Gion Matsuri features various cultural performances, including traditional music, dance, and theater, celebrating Kyoto's artistic heritage.

Gion Matsuri is a testament to the intertwining of spirituality, tradition, and art in Japanese culture. It preserves ancient customs while engaging the community in a festive and vibrant celebration that reflects Kyoto's historical significance.

Shinto's Influence on Japanese Culture and Ethics: An Enduring Spiritual Legacy

Shinto has permeated every facet of Japanese culture and ethics, shaping the nation's identity, values, and way of life. This indigenous belief system, with its reverence for nature, ancestral spirits, and kami, has helped to shape Japan's history, arts, ethics, and societal norms.

Cultural Landscape:

1. **Nature Aesthetics:** Shinto's emphasis on the sacredness of nature has profoundly influenced Japanese aesthetics. This influence is evident in the delicate art of bonsai, the tranquil landscapes of traditional gardens, and the concept of "wabi-sabi," celebrating the beauty of imperfection.

2. **Architecture:** Shinto shrines and their distinctive architectural styles, characterized by wooden structures, torii gates, and minimalist designs, have inspired Japanese architectural traditions. These elements can be seen in both traditional and modern buildings.

3. **Festivals and Celebrations:** Shinto festivals mark key moments in the calendar. Festivals like Tanabata and Setsubun reflect a blend of cultural and spiritual significance, fostering a sense of community and shared identity.

Ethical Foundations:

1. **Harmony with Nature:** Shinto's reverence for nature translates into an ethic of harmonious coexistence with the environment. This respect for the natural world is evident in sustainable practices, conservation efforts, and an understanding of humanity's interconnectedness with all living beings.

2. **Ancestor Veneration:** Ancestral veneration in Shinto underscores the importance of familial bonds and respect for elders. This ethic is embedded in Japanese values of filial piety, gratitude, and the passing down of traditions.

3. **Collectivism:** Shinto's influence can be seen in Japan's emphasis on group harmony, cooperation, and loyalty. The concept of "wa" (harmony) underscores the importance of preserving social equilibrium for the greater good.

Influences on Literature and Arts:

1. **Literature:** Shinto themes and beliefs have been woven into classical Japanese literature, such as "Kojiki" and "Nihon Shoki," both of which chronicle the nation's mythology and history.

2. **Performing Arts:** Noh theater, kabuki, and other traditional performing arts often draw inspiration from Shinto narratives and spiritual themes. The performing arts serve as vehicles for conveying cultural and spiritual messages.

Societal Norms:

1. **Respect for Elders and Tradition:** Shinto's emphasis on ancestral reverence reinforces the importance of respecting elders and traditional values in Japanese society.

2. **Social Harmony:** Shinto's focus on maintaining harmony with the divine and natural world resonates with Japan's societal emphasis on maintaining social harmony and order.

Shinto and Coexistence with Other Religions: Balancing Traditions in a Diverse Landscape

Shinto, Japan's indigenous spiritual tradition, has navigated a complex landscape of coexistence with various religious beliefs. As a religion deeply tied to the cultural identity of Japan, Shinto has demonstrated both adaptability and resilience in its interactions with other faiths, contributing to the unique religious landscape of the country.

Historical Interactions:

1. **Influence of Buddhism:** Shinto and Buddhism have coexisted in Japan for centuries. During the introduction of Buddhism to Japan, elements of both faiths intermingled. This syncretic approach led to the development of religious practices and festivals that incorporate elements of both traditions.

2. **Shugendo and Folk Beliefs:** Shugendo, a Japanese spiritual practice, blended elements of Shinto, Buddhism, and Taoism. This fusion reflected the fluidity and openness of Japanese spirituality, allowing for the integration of diverse influences.

Syncretism and Integration:

1. **Shared Shrines and Temples:** Many shrines and temples in Japan have shared grounds, a testament to the harmonious coexistence of different faiths. This practice, known as "jingu-ji," exemplifies the ability of Shinto and Buddhism to peacefully exist side by side.

2. **Obon Festival:** The Obon festival, celebrating ancestral spirits, is a prime example of syncretism. While rooted in Buddhism, it incorporates Shinto elements and exemplifies the blending of different beliefs.

Respectful Coexistence:

1. **Interfaith Dialogues:** Shinto, along with other religious communities, has participated in interfaith dialogues aimed at fostering mutual understanding and respect. These conversations aim to highlight shared values and promote peaceful coexistence.

2. **Shared Cultural Heritage:** Shinto and Buddhism have shared cultural symbols and practices that extend beyond religious boundaries. Concepts like respect for nature, ancestral veneration, and meditation are common threads that weave through both traditions.

With increased globalization, diverse religious communities interact more frequently. Shinto continues to adapt by fostering open conversations while retaining its unique identity. Japan's religious landscape exemplifies religious tolerance, allowing individuals to practice multiple faiths without contradiction. This acceptance is an embodiment of Shinto's historical openness to integrating various beliefs.

Shinto's coexistence with other religions underscores its adaptive and inclusive nature. Rather than isolating itself, Shinto has embraced and integrated various influences, shaping a religious landscape marked by diversity and harmonious interaction. This coexistence, characterized by shared spaces, cultural fusion, and interfaith dialogue, demonstrates how a deep respect for different beliefs can lead to the harmonious existence of faiths in a modern world.

Chapter 9

Jainism

Rooted in ancient India, this profound tradition offers a unique perspective on existence, emphasizing the interconnectedness of all living beings and the pursuit of liberation through ethical living. Through its teachings of non-harm, self-discipline, and the pursuit of truth, Jainism offers a transformative lens through which to view the world and our place within it.

Tirthankaras and Spiritual Liberation in Jainism: Ascending the Path of Enlightenment

At the core of Jainism, an ancient spiritual tradition that emerged in India, lies the profound concept of Tirthankaras—the enlightened beings who guide humanity toward spiritual liberation. Rooted in the pursuit of truth, non-violence, and ethical living, Jainism offers a path that seeks to break the cycle of suffering and attain ultimate liberation, known as "moksha." The Tirthankaras serve as beacons of wisdom and compassion, illuminating the transformative journey from ignorance to enlightenment.

Tirthankaras: Enlightened Spiritual Guides:

Tirthankaras are revered as enlightened souls who have achieved the pinnacle of spiritual realization. They are considered the spiritual leaders and role models for Jain followers, exemplifying the highest ideals of non-violence, truth, and detachment.

Attributes of Tirthankaras:

1. **Kevala Jnana:** Tirthankaras possess Kevala Jnana, a state of infinite knowledge that transcends time and space. This supreme wisdom allows them to understand the intricate workings of the universe, the cycle of birth and death, and the essence of reality.

2. **Renunciation:** Before attaining enlightenment, Tirthankaras lead lives of asceticism and renunciation, shedding attachments to material possessions, desires, and ego. Their journey exemplifies the pursuit of self-realization through self-discipline.

3. **Compassion:** Tirthankaras radiate boundless compassion and empathy for all living beings. Their teachings emphasize the significance of non-violence (ahimsa) and the interconnectedness of all life forms.

Cycle of Tirthankaras:

Jain cosmology envisions an endless cycle of Tirthankaras, each emerging to guide humanity during different eras. Twenty-four Tirthankaras are recognized in the present cosmic age. Lord Rishabhanatha, Lord Mahavira, and Lord Parshvanatha are among the most revered Tirthankaras, with Lord Mahavira being the 24th and most recent Tirthankara.

Jainism's ultimate goal is to attain moksha—the liberation of the soul from the cycle of birth and death (samsara). Achieving moksha involves transcending the bonds of karma—accumulated actions and their consequences—through rigorous spiritual practices and self-purification.

Pathways to Moksha:

1. **Right Belief:** Acquiring correct spiritual knowledge and understanding the nature of reality and the soul's true nature are fundamental to the path of moksha.

2. **Right Conduct:** Ethical behavior, marked by non-violence, truthfulness, non-stealing, chastity, and non-possessiveness, paves the way for the soul's purification.

3. **Right Knowledge:** Developing an intuitive understanding of the interconnectedness of the universe and the soul's detachment from worldly desires fosters a state of equanimity and detachment.

The pursuit of moksha extends beyond individual salvation. Jainism's emphasis on compassion and non-violence extends to the treatment of all living beings and the environment. The pursuit of ethical living is not only a means of personal liberation but also a way to create a harmonious and just society.

Principles of Non-Violence and Non-Possession in Jainism: Navigating the Path of Ahimsa and Aparigraha

At the heart of Jainism are two profound principles that have shaped its ethical foundation: "ahimsa" and "aparigraha." These principles advocate non-violence and non-possession, guiding adherents toward a life of compassion, self-discipline, and detachment. Rooted in the belief of the inherent value of all life forms and the transient nature of material possessions, these principles offer a transformative lens through which Jains navigate the complexities of existence.

Ahimsa: The Radiant Jewel of Non-Violence:

Ahimsa, often translated as non-violence, encompasses more than abstaining from physical harm. It extends to the realms of thoughts, words, and actions, promoting a profound respect for all living beings, regardless of their form or size.

Ahimsa is the cornerstone of Jain ethics, influencing personal conduct, dietary choices, relationships, and interactions with the environment. It reflects the deep understanding that every sentient being possesses a divine spark and deserves to be treated with compassion.

Practice of Ahimsa:

1. **Non-Injury:** Jains consciously avoid causing harm to any living being, refraining from violence, aggression, or harm in thought, word, or deed.

2. **Vegan Lifestyle:** Many Jains adopt a strict vegan lifestyle to minimize harm to animals. This involves avoiding all animal products, including meat, dairy, and even certain root vegetables.

3. **Mindful Speech:** Practicing ahimsa involves speaking truthfully, kindly, and in ways that do not cause pain or harm to others. Gossip, harsh language, and verbal aggression are avoided.

4. **Thought Control:** Jains also strive to cultivate a mind free from violent thoughts, anger, and negative emotions.

Aparigraha: The Art of Non-Possession:

Aparigraha, often translated as non-possession or non-attachment, emphasizes detachment from material possessions and the transient nature of worldly belongings.

Aparigraha encourages individuals to limit their desires and attachments, recognizing that material possessions can hinder spiritual progress and lead to suffering.

Practice of Aparigraha:

1. **Minimalism:** Jains adopt a minimalist lifestyle, owning only what is necessary for sustenance and survival.

2. **Renunciation:** Some Jain ascetics, known as monks and nuns, take aparigraha to its highest expression by relinquishing all personal possessions and living a life of complete detachment.

3. **Economic Ethics:** Jain business practices emphasize honesty, fair trade, and ethical financial dealings, aligning with the principles of non-possession.

The principles of ahimsa and aparigraha shape the personal character of Jains, fostering qualities such as compassion, humility, and contentment. By promoting non-violence and non-possession, Jains contribute to creating a more compassionate and harmonious society.

Ethical Pillars Guiding Life:

Ahimsa and aparigraha stand as pillars of ethical living in Jainism, embodying the ideals of compassion and detachment. These principles offer a profound way to engage with the world—one that respects the intrinsic value of all life forms and acknowledges the transient nature of material possessions. By adhering to these principles, Jains aspire to cultivate inner peace, harmonious relationships, and a deep understanding of the interconnectedness of all beings—an approach to life that beckons us to embrace compassion and let go of attachments as we navigate the journey of existence.

Ahimsa and Ethical Conduct: The Compassionate Path of Non-Violence in Jainism

In the heart of Jainism's ethical framework beats the principle of "ahimsa," an ancient Sanskrit term that signifies non-violence in thought, word, and action. Ahimsa is not just about not causing physical harm; it is a philosophy that extends compassion and respect to all sentient beings. It forms the bedrock of Jain ethical conduct, influencing every facet of life and fostering a deep understanding of the interconnectedness of all existence.

Ahimsa's Scope and Significance:

- **Thought, Word, and Deed:** Ahimsa encompasses three realms: "manasika" (thought), "vachika" (speech), and "kayika" (action). It promotes non-violence at each level, recognizing the power of words and intentions to cause harm.
- **Inherent Value of Life:** At the core of ahimsa is the belief that every living being possesses inherent value. Jains extend compassion even to the tiniest of creatures, considering all life forms as potential vessels of divinity.

Principles and Practices:

- **Non-Injury:** The cornerstone of ahimsa is refraining from causing harm to any being, whether through physical violence, emotional harm, or mental agitation.
- **Vegan Lifestyle:** Ahimsa often leads Jains to adopt a vegan diet, avoiding all forms of animal products to minimize harm to sentient beings.

- **Mindful Communication:** Practicing ahimsa in speech involves speaking truthfully, kindly, and without causing harm. Gossip, harsh words, and divisive language are discouraged.
- **Internal Harmony:** Ahimsa encourages inner peace and mental tranquility by promoting thoughts of love, compassion, and empathy.

Challenges and Ethical Dilemmas:

- **Dietary Choices:** Jains navigate the challenge of adhering to a vegan lifestyle while respecting local customs and food availability.
- **Self-Defense:** The principle of ahimsa raises questions about self-defense and protection when facing potential harm.
- **Modern World:** In a world filled with complex systems that may indirectly contribute to harm, Jains strive to find ways to minimize harm while maintaining practicality.

Ahimsa in Action:

- **Business Ethics:** Jain businesspersons emphasize ethical trade, fair dealings, and ensuring that their activities do not contribute to violence or exploitation.
- **Environmental Responsibility:** Ahimsa extends to environmental stewardship, promoting sustainable practices and the reduction of ecological impact.
- **Social Activism:** Jains engage in non-violent social activism to address issues like animal cruelty, environmental degradation, and human rights.

Ascetic Practices and the Path to Salvation in Jainism: Transcending the Worldly Bonds

In the intricate tapestry of Jainism, the path to salvation, or "moksha," is woven with the threads of rigorous practices. Jainism offers a distinct approach to attaining liberation by shedding the shackles of karma and realizing the pure nature of the soul.

Asceticism as a Pillar of Jainism:

Ascetic practices are rooted in the understanding that worldly attachments, desires, and possessions perpetuate the cycle of karma and suffering. By renouncing these ties, practitioners aim to liberate themselves from the entanglements of material life.

Stages of Spiritual Ascent:

1. **Householder (Shravaka):** In this initial stage, followers focus on ethical living, non-violence, and the study of Jain scriptures.
2. **Initiation into Asceticism:** Devotees who yearn for a deeper spiritual commitment undergo initiation as monks (sadhus) or nuns (sadhvis), embracing an ascetic lifestyle.
3. **Monastic Life:** Ascetics live lives of minimalism, simplicity, and self-control. They give up all personal possessions, wear simple white robes, and adhere to strict vows.

Five Great Vows (Mahavratas):

1. **Non-Violence (Ahimsa):** The core of Jain ethics, non-violence extends to not causing harm in thought, word, or action. Ascetics meticulously avoid harming any living being.
2. **Truthfulness (Satya):** Ascetics commit to speaking truthfully, avoiding deceit, exaggeration, and manipulation.
3. **Non-Stealing (Asteya):** Ascetics refrain from taking what is not rightfully theirs, cultivating an attitude of contentment.

4. **Celibacy (Brahmacharya):** Ascetics embrace celibacy to transcend bodily desires and attain spiritual purity.

5. **Non-Possession (Aparigraha):** Ascetics relinquish all material possessions, practicing detachment from worldly attachments.

Rigorous Austerities (Tapas):

Ascetics practice austerities to purify the soul, burn off accumulated karma, and accelerate spiritual progress. These austerities range from fasting and meditation to controlling the senses and enduring physical hardships. This then leads to the path of liberation, including:

- **Breaking the Cycle of Karma:** Ascetic practices aim to reduce and eventually eliminate karma—the accumulated consequences of past actions—that binds the soul to the cycle of birth and death.

- **Spiritual Purity:** By practicing non-violence, truth, and other vows, ascetics cultivate inner purity, allowing them to transcend worldly distractions and focus on spiritual realization.

- **Self-Realization and Enlightenment:** Ascetics strive to attain higher knowledge (jñana) and direct perception (darshana) of the true nature of reality. This leads to self-realization and the eventual liberation of the soul.

Cultural Contributions and Contemporary Relevance of Jainism: Illuminating the Past, Guiding the Present

Jainism has contributed to culture, philosophy, and ethical living. Its teachings of non-violence, compassion, and detachment have not only enriched the spiritual landscape but also continue to resonate with contemporary society, offering valuable insights into navigating the complexities of modern life.

Literature and Philosophy:

1. **Jain Scriptures:** The Agamas, a collection of Jain scriptures, delve into cosmology, ethics, and spiritual practices. The Tattvartha Sutra provides a comprehensive philosophical framework that has influenced Indian philosophy.

2. **Influences on Indian Philosophy:** Jainism's emphasis on pluralism, non-violence, and the nature of reality has contributed to the broader philosophical discourse in India.

Art and Architecture:

1. **Intricate Temples:** Jain temples are renowned for their exquisite architectural details and intricate carvings. These temples are not just places of worship but also artistic masterpieces.

2. **Symbolism:** Jain art often features symbols such as the swastika and the Jain hand gesture, representing well-being, non-violence, and spiritual aspirations.

Ethics and Environmental Stewardship:

1. **Non-Violence and Animal Welfare:** Jainism's commitment to non-violence has relevance in today's discussions on animal rights, veganism, and ethical treatment of animals.

2. **Environmental Responsibility:** Jain teachings of non-possession and non-violence naturally align with the urgency of ecological conservation and sustainable living

Non-Violence and Conflict Resolution:

1. **Global Relevance:** The principle of non-violence has inspired global figures like Mahatma Gandhi and Dr. Martin Luther King Jr., impacting movements for civil rights and social justice.

2. **Conflict Resolution:** Jain principles of dialogue, empathy, and non-violence offer practical solutions for resolving conflicts without aggression.

Simplicity and Materialism:

1. **Minimalism:** Jain ascetic practices and emphasis on non-possession reflect contemporary discussions on minimalism and reducing consumerism.

2. **Mental Health:** Jain teachings on detachment and contentment offer a perspective on combating stress and finding inner peace in an age of material excess.

Interfaith and Social Harmony:

1. **Interfaith Dialogue:** Jainism's inclusivity and respect for all life forms contribute to interfaith dialogues, fostering understanding among different belief systems.

2. **Social Integration:** Jain philanthropic efforts, such as providing food and medical aid, highlight the tradition's commitment to social welfare.

In a world grappling with environmental challenges, ethical dilemmas, and the need for compassion, Jainism's teachings on non-violence, detachment, and empathy offer profound guidance. Its relevance is felt not only in personal lives but also in the broader realms of ethical governance, social justice, and ecological sustainability.

As a beacon of wisdom, Jainism shines light on a path that navigates the complexities of contemporary existence while reminding us of the enduring importance of values that transcend time and place.

Chapter 10

Confucianism

Confucianism, an ancient and influential philosophical and ethical system, is built upon a foundation of core principles and values that have shaped the way people think and interact in East Asian societies for centuries.

At its heart are five essential virtues that provide guidance for personal conduct, social relationships, and moral decision-making.

1. **Ren (Benevolence):** At the forefront of Confucian values stands "Ren," which embodies the idea of kindness, compassion, and empathy toward others. It's the cornerstone of harmonious relationships and encourages us to treat everyone with genuine care and consideration. By practicing Ren, individuals contribute to a society characterized by understanding and goodwill.

2. **Li (Rituals and Etiquette):** "Li" emphasizes the importance of rituals, customs, and proper behavior. It's not about mere formality, but rather about using rituals to cultivate respect and order in our interactions. Through observing Li, we express our commitment to social harmony and demonstrate our understanding of the roles and responsibilities we hold in various relationships.

3. **Xiao (Filial Piety):** "Xiao" revolves around the concept of honoring and respecting one's parents and ancestors. It extends beyond just family, emphasizing the reverence we owe to those who came before us. By upholding Xiao, we strengthen the bonds within our families and reinforce the intergenerational connections that enrich our culture.

4. **Yi (Righteousness):** "Yi" guides us in making morally upright decisions. It urges us to act ethically and justly, even in the face of challenges or temptations. This virtue champions the idea that doing what is right should always take precedence, contributing to a fair and virtuous society where everyone can trust in the integrity of others.

5. **Zhi (Wisdom):** The fifth virtue, "Zhi," underscores the value of wisdom and knowledge. It encourages lifelong learning and the pursuit of understanding. By cultivating wisdom, we not only enrich our own lives but also contribute to the betterment of society as our insights and knowledge are shared with others.

These Confucian principles collectively create a roadmap for individuals to lead meaningful and harmonious lives within their communities. They shape personal character, guide decision-making, and foster a sense of responsibility toward others. While deeply rooted in historical contexts, these values remain relevant today, inspiring people to cultivate virtues that promote empathy, respect, and a sense of purpose.

Whether applied in family dynamics, educational endeavors, or societal interactions, the core principles of Confucianism continue to influence cultures and guide individuals toward a more compassionate and balanced way of life.

Social Harmony and Order in Confucianism: Balancing Relationships and Roles

In Confucian thought, one of the most intricate and enduring threads is the emphasis on social harmony and order. Rooted in ancient China, Confucianism places a profound significance on maintaining equilibrium within society through well-defined relationships, ethical behavior, and a sense of responsibility. This intricate web of interconnections has not only shaped East Asian cultures but also offers valuable insights into building harmonious societies worldwide.

The Five Relationships: Foundations of Harmony

At the heart of Confucian social philosophy are the Five Relationships, which lay the groundwork for harmonious interactions and balanced social order. These relationships establish a hierarchy that encompasses various facets of life:

1. **Ruler and Subject:** This relationship centers on the proper conduct of governance, where rulers are responsible for benevolent leadership, and subjects owe loyalty and obedience in return.

2. **Father and Son:** Within the family sphere, this relationship signifies the nurturing role of parents and the filial piety expected from children. Respect for parents and ancestors is an essential thread that weaves through generations.

3. **Husband and Wife:** The bond between spouses is built on mutual respect and support. Harmony in this relationship is

achieved through shared responsibilities and understanding, rather than dominance.

4. **Older and Younger Sibling:** Sibling relationships echo the principle of respect for elders and guidance for younger siblings. This dynamic fosters cooperation and mentorship within families.

5. **Friend and Friend:** Although not hierarchical, friendship holds its place in Confucianism. Friends support one another morally and ethically, promoting virtuous conduct in society.

Rituals, Etiquette, and Moral Behavior

Confucianism considers rituals (Li) and proper etiquette to be essential tools for cultivating social harmony. These rituals extend beyond mere formalities; they represent respect for tradition and each other. By adhering to rituals, individuals express their roles and responsibilities, fostering an environment of mutual understanding and respect.

In Confucian thought, the family serves as the nucleus of societal harmony. Filial piety (Xiao) is a cornerstone virtue that strengthens familial bonds, and these bonds extend outward, influencing community relationships. The emphasis on family-centered values helps establish a strong foundation for social cohesion, as individuals carry these values into their interactions beyond the home.

The Moral Imperative of Self-Cultivation

A central tenet of Confucianism is the pursuit of self-cultivation and personal improvement. By refining themselves morally and intellectually, individuals contribute positively to the larger societal fabric. Wisdom (Zhi) and righteousness (Yi) guide individuals to make ethical decisions that align with the well-being of the community.

Confucian ideals of social harmony face both praise and critique in modern times. While they foster stability and cooperation, critics argue that these ideals can also stifle individuality and discourage questioning authority. Gender roles within these relationships have also come under scrutiny for perpetuating inequality. Nevertheless, the adaptability of Confucianism has allowed its principles to persist and evolve in the face of changing social landscapes.

Educational Philosophy in Confucianism: Nurturing Virtuous Leaders

Confucianism, beyond its ethical and societal principles, lays a strong foundation for educational philosophy that has greatly influenced East Asian cultures. Rooted in the belief that education is not merely a tool for acquiring knowledge, but a means to cultivate virtuous individuals and responsible citizens, Confucian educational ideals have left an indelible mark on education systems, emphasizing character development, lifelong learning, and social contribution.

Central to Confucian education is the belief that the primary goal of learning is the refinement of a person's character. While knowledge is valued, it is considered secondary to the development of virtues such as benevolence (Ren), righteousness (Yi), and wisdom (Zhi). Students are encouraged to internalize these virtues through their studies and interactions, thereby becoming morally upright individuals who contribute positively to society.

In Confucian educational philosophy, the teacher holds a revered position. The teacher is not merely an instructor of facts, but a moral guide who imparts wisdom, fosters respect for tradition, and nurtures students' growth as responsible members of society. This mentorship model emphasizes the importance of strong teacher-student relationships, characterized by mutual respect and a commitment to both academic and ethical development.

Emphasis on Rituals and Etiquette

Confucian education emphasizes the teaching of rituals (Li) and proper behavior. By engaging in rituals and observing proper etiquette, students learn to navigate social relationships with grace and respect. These practices instill an understanding of social roles, hierarchy, and the importance of harmony in interactions.

Learning is seen as a lifelong journey. This belief stems from the idea that growth and self-cultivation do not have an endpoint but are ongoing pursuits. Students are encouraged to remain curious, open-minded, and committed to self-improvement throughout their lives. This philosophy aligns with the Confucian concept of wisdom (Zhi), which acknowledges that true wisdom comes from a continuous pursuit of knowledge and self-reflection.

Educational Hierarchy and Social Mobility

Confucian education historically operated within a hierarchical structure, often linked to social status and privilege. However, it also held the potential for social mobility. The idea that individuals could rise through the ranks of society through education allowed for a meritocratic approach, emphasizing that virtue and ability, rather than birth, should determine one's position in society.

While Confucian educational philosophy has timeless virtues, it also faces challenges in modern times. Critics argue that its emphasis on conformity and rote learning can stifle creativity and critical thinking. Additionally, gender bias within traditional Confucian values has been a point of contention. In response, contemporary educational approaches seek to balance Confucian ideals with modern pedagogical methods that promote holistic development, critical thinking, and inclusivity.

Cultural Influence of Confucianism: Shaping East Asian Societies

Confucianism has woven itself into the cultural fabric of East Asian societies, leaving an enduring impact on various aspects of life. From governance and family dynamics to art and literature, Confucian principles have shaped values, norms, and traditions across centuries, contributing to the distinct identities of nations such as China, Japan, South Korea, and Vietnam.

Its influence on governance is evident in its emphasis on benevolent leadership and social harmony. The teachings of Confucius advocate for rulers who prioritize the well-being of their subjects and adhere to moral principles. This philosophy has historically guided the formation of bureaucratic systems, with officials selected based on merit rather than birth, reflecting a form of meritocracy.

Family as the Cornerstone of Society

The family-oriented values of Confucianism have left an indelible mark on the structure of East Asian societies. Filial piety (Xiao), emphasizing respect for parents and ancestors, extends beyond individual households to foster collective familial bonds. This reverence for familial ties has reinforced a sense of duty and responsibility, shaping family structures and interactions.

Education as a Moral Imperative

Confucianism's educational philosophy has heavily influenced the approach to learning in East Asia. Education is not solely about knowledge acquisition; it's a means to cultivate virtues and character. This perspective has led to a cultural appreciation for scholarship, with societies placing high value on formal education and continuous self-improvement.

Cultural Expressions: Art, Literature, and Rituals

Confucian ideals are deeply embedded in various cultural expressions. Traditional art often portrays scenes of respect, harmony, and hierarchy, mirroring Confucian principles. Literary works frequently explore moral dilemmas, ethical choices, and the complexities of human relationships, influenced by Confucian thought. Rituals and ceremonies uphold Confucian values and maintain social order, permeating life's milestones and public events.

Work Ethics and Social Etiquette

Confucian principles have also influenced work ethics and social etiquette. Concepts of diligence, responsibility, and dedication are rooted in the teachings of Confucius. Respectful behavior, such as bowing, addressing elders with honorifics, and using appropriate language, reflects the emphasis on maintaining social harmony and adhering to proper conduct.

Continuity and Adaptation

Throughout history, Confucianism has adapted to changing contexts while retaining its core values. It has survived political shifts, cultural transformations, and technological advancements, testament to its resilience and adaptability. Even as East Asian societies modernize, Confucian values continue to shape moral outlooks, decision-making, and cultural practices.

Adaptation and Critique of Confucianism: Navigating Tradition and Change

Confucianism has encountered both adaptation and critique as it navigates the complex terrain of tradition and contemporary realities. As societies evolve and cultures transform, Confucian values have been examined, challenged, and reinterpreted to remain relevant in a changing world. This interplay between adaptation and critique reflects the dynamic nature of this influential philosophical system.

One of Confucianism's remarkable attributes is its ability to adapt without compromising its core principles. In response to modernization, Confucianism has found new ways to resonate with contemporary societies:

1. **Gender Equality:** Traditional Confucian values often contained gender biases, assigning specific roles and responsibilities to men and women. Modern interpretations seek to address these imbalances, promoting gender equality and inclusivity.

2. **Human Rights:** The emphasis on hierarchy and social order in Confucianism has been critiqued for potentially stifling individual rights. Contemporary adaptations aim to reconcile Confucian values with universal human rights, highlighting areas of overlap.

3. **Environmental Ethics:** As environmental concerns gain prominence, Confucian principles are being reinterpreted to incorporate ecological ethics. The emphasis on harmony and balance is being extended to the relationship between humans and nature.

4. **Global Relevance:** Confucianism's ethical values and emphasis on social harmony have transcended geographical boundaries. As East Asian cultures engage with the global community, Confucian principles are being explored as potential guides for cross-cultural understanding and cooperation.

As we have briefly mentioned, Confucianism has not been exempt from critique, as its traditional values are examined through modern lenses:

1. **Rigidity and Conformity:** Critics argue that Confucian emphasis on conformity and social hierarchy can suppress

individuality and discourage questioning of authority, hindering social progress and innovation.

2. **Gender Equality:** Traditional Confucian teachings often perpetuated gender inequality. Critics highlight the need for more inclusive interpretations that align with modern standards of gender equity.

3. **Cultural Conservatism:** Some assert that Confucianism's emphasis on tradition can hinder societal evolution, preventing adaptation to changing cultural and social norms.

4. **Modern Governance:** Critics contend that Confucian ideals of governance, while benevolent, might not fully address the complexities of modern political systems and global challenges.

Navigating the Balance: Contemporary Reinterpretations

The dialogue between adaptation and critique has led to a spectrum of reinterpretations that navigate the intricate balance between tradition and change:

1. **Progressive Confucianism:** This approach seeks to integrate Confucian values with contemporary ideas, addressing criticisms while preserving core ethical principles.

2. **Feminist Interpretations:** Scholars are reexamining Confucian texts to uncover overlooked narratives that can support gender equality and challenge traditional roles.

3. **Humanistic Confucianism:** Emphasizing the human-centered aspects of Confucianism, this perspective highlights values that align with universal human dignity and rights.

4. **Eco-Confucianism:** This adaptation seeks to harmonize Confucian values with environmental ethics, advocating for sustainable living and ecological awareness.

The adaptation and critique of Confucianism reflect its capacity to evolve while retaining its essence. As societies confront complex challenges and cultural shifts, Confucianism continues to engage in a dynamic process of reevaluation and adaptation, demonstrating its enduring relevance as a source of ethical guidance and social harmony.

Chapter 11

Taoism

Amidst the rich spiritual traditions, Taoism emerges as a serene and profound philosophy that beckons us to align ourselves with the natural rhythms of the universe. Originating in ancient China, Taoism encapsulates a profound understanding of balance, harmony, and the interconnectedness of all existence.

Through its teachings on the Tao, or the Way, Taoism invites us to embark on a journey of self-discovery, where simplicity, humility, and a deep reverence for the natural world guide us toward inner peace and a profound connection to the mysteries of existence.

Laozi and the Tao Te Ching: Navigating the Path of Inner Harmony

At the heart of Taoism stands Laozi, a legendary figure and the attributed author of the seminal text, the Tao Te Ching. Laozi's teachings have left a mark on the philosophy, spirituality, and ethical contemplation of Taoism. Through the Tao Te Ching, Laozi imparts profound insights that illuminate the path toward harmony, simplicity, and self-realization.

Laozi's life remains shrouded in mystery, but he is believed to have lived during the 6th century BCE in ancient China, a time of intellectual and philosophical ferment.

The name "Laozi" translates to "Old Master," hinting at his revered status as a wise sage. Legends suggest that Laozi was a humble archivist, who, disillusioned with societal corruption, embarked on a journey to seek enlightenment.

The Tao Te Ching: A Source of Eternal Wisdom:

Laozi's most influential legacy is the Tao Te Ching, a poetic and enigmatic work consisting of 81 short chapters. This text lays the philosophical foundation of Taoism and is considered one of the most translated and revered works in human history.

Central to the Tao Te Ching is the concept of the Tao, which signifies the ineffable force that flows through all things. Laozi urges individuals to align with the Tao, embracing the effortless spontaneity of nature.

Laozi emphasizes the principle of "wu wei," often translated as "effortless action" or "non-action." It suggests acting in harmony with the natural flow of events, avoiding unnecessary resistance.

Simplicity and Humility:

The Tao Te Ching advocates for a life of simplicity, free from excessive desires and material pursuits. Laozi encourages us to embrace the unadorned beauty of existence.

Laozi extols humility as the path to wisdom and inner peace. This humility, rooted in the recognition of one's connection to all beings, leads to compassion and harmony.

Inner Transformation:

Laozi's teachings invite individuals to embark on a journey of self-discovery, exploring the depths of their inner being and realizing their connection to the greater cosmos.

Laozi's philosophy encompasses the notion that opposites are interconnected and interdependent. This understanding challenges dualistic thinking and encourages a holistic perspective.

Legacy and Contemporary Relevance:

Laozi's teachings continue to serve as a spiritual compass, guiding individuals toward balance, tranquility, and a profound understanding of the mysteries of existence.

Beyond Taoism, Laozi's wisdom has resonated with philosophers, scholars, and thinkers across cultures, sparking reflections on the nature of reality, ethics, and the human condition.

Following the Way of Laozi:

Laozi, through his Tao Te Ching, offers a path of introspection and transformation that resonates with seekers of wisdom from every corner of the globe. His teachings remind us that in embracing the natural rhythms of existence, cultivating inner simplicity, and embodying humility, we align ourselves with the profound harmony that permeates the universe.

Concepts of Yin and Yang, and Wu Wei: Navigating the Taoist Path of Balance and Effortless Action

In the heart of Taoist philosophy lies a profound understanding of two fundamental concepts: yin and yang, and wu wei. These concepts serve as guiding principles for living in harmony with the natural order, fostering a balanced and harmonious existence that resonates with the rhythm of the cosmos. Through yin and yang, Taoism explores the dualities of existence, while wu wei offers a path to navigate life with grace and simplicity.

Yin and Yang: Balancing Dualities:

The concept of yin and yang encapsulates the interplay of dual forces—darkness and light, femininity and masculinity, contraction and expansion—that create the dynamic harmony of the universe.

Yin and yang are not opposing forces, but rather complementary and interdependent aspects that give rise to each other. They form a continuous cycle of change and transformation.

Taoism emphasizes the importance of maintaining balance between yin and yang. Harmony is achieved when these forces are in equilibrium, reflecting the harmony of nature itself.

Wu Wei: Effortless Action and Non-Action:

Wu wei, often translated as "effortless action" or "non-action," refers to acting in alignment with the natural flow of events. It is about letting go of resistance and allowing things to unfold organically. It does not imply passivity, laziness, or indifference. Rather, it is a state of deep attentiveness and alignment with the underlying currents of life.

In essence, wu wei encourages individuals to transcend ego-driven desires and attachments, allowing the innate intelligence of the universe to guide their actions.

Cultivation of Virtue:

Wu wei requires a deep understanding of the inner self and a continuous cultivation of virtues such as humility, compassion, and selflessness.

Through practicing wu wei, individuals develop an intuitive sense of when to act and when to refrain from action. This intuitive response arises from a state of heightened awareness.

By embodying the principles of yin and yang and embracing the concept of wu wei, individuals harmonize their inner world with the outer world, leading to a life of greater tranquility, authenticity, and alignment with the Tao.

Contemporary Relevance:

The concepts of yin and yang and wu wei offer insights into navigating the complexities of modern life, fostering resilience and adaptability in an ever-changing world.

Wu wei encourages mindfulness and conscious decision-making, making it relevant to practices such as mindfulness meditation and sustainable living.

Embracing the Taoist Way:

The concepts of yin and yang and wu wei unveil a profound philosophy that speaks to the depth of human existence. Through their exploration, Taoism offers a unique perspective on the duality of life, the interconnectedness of all things, and the art of living in harmony with the natural order. By embracing the balance of yin and yang and practicing the art of wu wei, individuals embark on a transformative journey, aligning themselves with the flow of the universe and discovering the beauty of effortless action—a path that leads to a profound sense of peace, authenticity, and unity with the Tao.

Immortality and Spiritual Harmony in Taoism: Seeking the Elixir of Transcendence

Within the realm of Taoism, the quest for immortality and spiritual harmony is a driving force, guiding seekers toward a state of profound union with the Tao—the ultimate reality that underlies all existence. This aspiration isn't merely about achieving physical immortality, but rather, it symbolizes the transcendence of ego, the alignment with cosmic rhythms, and the realization of one's intrinsic connection to the universe.

Concepts of Immortality:

Taoist texts often describe various methods to achieve both physical and spiritual immortality. While the former seeks to prolong physical life, the latter transcends the limitations of the physical body.

Ancient Taoist alchemical practices centered around the quest for the "Elixir of Life," a metaphorical substance representing spiritual enlightenment and the attainment of immortality.

True immortality, according to Taoism, is achieved by aligning one's essence with the Tao. This leads to a state of spiritual harmony that transcends the cycles of birth and death.

The Path of Spiritual Harmony:

Spiritual harmony is attained by relinquishing attachments to material desires, ego, and external validations. This paves the way for an inner state of tranquility and freedom.

Taoism emphasizes the cultivation of virtues such as humility, compassion, and simplicity. These virtues harmonize the individual's inner state with the natural order.

Inner alchemy is a spiritual practice within Taoism that involves transforming one's inner energies to achieve spiritual enlightenment.

It's a process of refining one's consciousness and aligning it with the Tao.

Union with Nature:

Immortality and spiritual harmony are intertwined with the harmonious relationship between humanity and the natural world. By emulating the simplicity and balance of nature, individuals harmonize with the Tao.

The Taoist sage embodies the ideal of spiritual harmony and immortality. Sages are in tune with the Tao, living in accordance with the natural way of life.

Beyond Mortality, Toward Unity:

In Taoism, the quest for immortality and spiritual harmony is a journey of profound significance. It transcends the boundaries of physical existence, inviting individuals to explore the depths of their consciousness, cultivate virtues, and align themselves with the timeless wisdom of the Tao.

Through this quest, seekers strive to harmonize with the universe, embody the virtues of the sage, and realize the interconnectedness of all things. As the journey unfolds, the search for immortality evolves into an embrace of the eternal—a unity that resonates with the rhythms of existence, propelling individuals toward a state of enduring peace, harmony, and oneness with the cosmos.

Practices: Qigong and Feng Shui - Harmonizing Body and Environment in Taoism

Taoism isn't merely a philosophy to be contemplated; it's a way of life to be embodied. This embodiment finds expression through practices like Qigong and Feng Shui, each offering a unique avenue to cultivate physical well-being and harmonize with the surrounding environment. Rooted in Taoist principles, these practices serve as pathways to balance, vitality, and a profound connection to the rhythms of existence.

Qigong: Nurturing Vital Energy and Inner Balance:

Qigong, often translated as "energy cultivation," is a holistic practice that combines breath, movement, meditation, and visualization. It aims to balance the flow of vital energy (qi) within the body.

Central to Qigong is the harmonization of qi, the life force that animates all living things. Through specific postures and gentle movements, practitioners clear blockages and allow qi to flow freely.

Qigong promotes physical health by enhancing circulation, boosting the immune system, and reducing stress. It's believed that aligning with the Tao through Qigong contributes to a longer and healthier life. It also aligns with Taoist principles of inner alchemy, the transformation of one's inner energies to attain spiritual enlightenment. By cultivating and refining qi, practitioners nourish their inner being.

Feng Shui: Harmony in Environmental Design:

Feng Shui, meaning "wind" and "water," is an ancient Chinese practice that harmonizes the environment with the flow of energy. It involves the strategic arrangement of spaces to optimize positive energy (chi) flow.

The practice seeks to achieve a balance between yin and yang energies within a space. By harmonizing these forces, practitioners create environments that support well-being and prosperity.

The Bagua map is a fundamental tool in Feng Shui that divides a space into eight sections, each corresponding to different life aspects. By aligning objects and features with the Bagua map, practitioners create an environment that supports their intentions.

In addition, Feng Shui offers practical techniques for enhancing the energy of a space, such as incorporating natural elements, optimizing lighting, and using colors that resonate with the intended purpose of the space.

Balancing Within and Without:

Qigong and Feng Shui are practical embodiments of Taoist principles, guiding people toward harmonious living within themselves and in their surroundings. By cultivating vital energy through Qigong and harmonizing their environments through Feng Shui, practitioners tap into the timeless wisdom of the Tao.

These practices remind us that the journey to balance and harmony isn't confined to philosophical musings; it's woven into the fabric of our daily lives. As we engage in these practices, we walk the path of Taoism, aligning with the rhythms of the universe, and nurturing the well-being of body, mind, and spirit.

Influence of Taoism on Chinese Philosophy and Culture: Nurturing the Soul of the Nation

Taoism, with its profound insights and holistic worldview, has permeated the very fabric of Chinese philosophy and culture for over two millennia. Its teachings affected the way individuals perceive the world, interact with nature, and cultivate their inner lives. As one of China's foundational spiritual traditions, Taoism's influence extends beyond its philosophical concepts, shaping art, literature, ethics, and even governance.

Shaping Chinese Philosophy:

Taoism's concept of yin and yang, the harmonious interplay of opposites, has also found its way into Confucian thought. It complements Confucian ethics by emphasizing the balance between opposing forces in maintaining harmony.

In addition, Taoist notions of aligning with the natural order and the importance of simplicity have resonated with Neo-Confucian philosophers who sought to achieve harmony between human beings and the cosmos.

While Taoist philosophy's exploration of the profound mysteries of existence has enriched Chinese philosophical discourse, inviting a contemplation of metaphysical questions resonate with the inquisitive nature of Chinese thinkers.

Cultural Expressions:

- **Art and Aesthetics:** Taoism's reverence for nature and the ineffable has inspired Chinese artists to create works that capture the essence of the natural world, leading to the development of nature-oriented aesthetics.
- **Literature and Poetry:** Taoist themes frequently appear in Chinese literature and poetry, often used to convey spiritual insights, introspection, and a deep sense of connectedness to the universe.
- **Calligraphy and Symbols:** Taoist symbols, such as the yin-yang symbol and the Bagua, are embedded in calligraphy, architecture, and traditional Chinese medicine, reflecting the integration of Taoist wisdom into daily life.

Taoist virtues, particularly humility and compassion, have deeply influenced Chinese moral values and ethical conduct. The emphasis on simplicity and contentment advocated by Taoism has found resonance in the Chinese cultural preference for minimalism and frugality.

Impact on Governance:

The Taoist concept of wu wei, or non-action, has guided rulers in understanding the art of governance—knowing when to act and when to let things unfold naturally.

Also, the emphasis on harmony and balance has contributed to Chinese political philosophy, encouraging leaders to maintain equilibrium between authority and the well-being of the people.

The influence of Taoism on Chinese philosophy and culture is akin to threads woven intricately into a vibrant tapestry. Its principles of balance, harmony, and alignment with the Tao have shaped the way individuals perceive their role in the cosmos, the way they govern, create, and live.

Through the centuries, Taoism has not only contributed to the richness of Chinese thought but has also transcended cultural boundaries, offering universal insights that resonate with the depths of the human experience. As China continues to evolve, the enduring legacy of Taoism serves as a reminder of the timeless wisdom that guides individuals in their quest for meaning, connection, and spiritual fulfillment.

Chapter 12

Zoroastrianism

Rooted in the teachings of the prophet Zoroaster, this enigmatic faith has illuminated the hearts and minds of its followers for millennia. With its profound belief in the cosmic battle between opposing forces, Zoroastrianism unveils a unique perspective on the human journey, where the pursuit of righteousness and the quest for enlightenment intertwine to shape a path of virtue, devotion, and the eternal pursuit of the ultimate truth.

Prophet Zoroaster (Zarathustra): Catalyst of Zoroastrian Revelation

At the heart of Zoroastrianism stands the prophetic figure of Zoroaster, also known as Zarathustra. Born in ancient Persia, possibly during the 6th or 7th century BCE, Zoroaster's life and teachings have left a mark on the religious and philosophical landscape of human history. His visionary insights and revelations form the foundation of one of the world's oldest monotheistic religions—Zoroastrianism.

According to Zoroastrian tradition, Zoroaster experienced a series of divine visions and conversations with Ahura Mazda, the supreme deity. These revelations shaped his understanding of the cosmic battle between the forces of good and evil.

Zoroaster's teachings are preserved in the Gathas, a collection of hymns composed in an ancient Iranian language. These hymns capture his theological insights, ethical principles, and reflections on the nature of existence.

His most distinctive contribution to world thought is his concept of cosmic dualism. He identified Ahura Mazda as the embodiment of truth, order, and light, while Angra Mainyu (Ahriman) represented falsehood, chaos, and darkness.

Zoroaster's teachings revolve around the eternal battle between these opposing forces, where humanity's choices play a crucial role in determining the outcome of this cosmic conflict.

Ethical Foundations:

Zoroaster emphasized ethical conduct, prescribing a set of principles that guided individuals toward righteousness, truthfulness, and compassion. His teachings fostered a sense of responsibility for one's choices and their impact on the world.

He introduced the concept of a final judgment, where each soul would face a reckoning for its actions. The righteous would be rewarded in the afterlife, while the wicked would face punishment.

Zoroaster's teachings found resonance within the Achaemenid Empire, where Zoroastrianism became the state religion. His ethical principles influenced the governance and administration of the empire.

Scholars believe that Zoroastrian ideas, particularly the concepts of judgment and dualism, may have influenced later monotheistic religions such as Judaism and Christianity. Despite challenges, Zoroastrianism persists in pockets around the world, particularly in India and Iran. Its teachings continue to inspire seekers of truth and meaning.

Dualistic Worldview in Zoroastrianism: The Eternal Battle of Good vs. Evil

At the core of Zoroastrianism lies a profound dualistic worldview that shapes its understanding of existence, morality, and the cosmic order. This dualism, rooted in the teachings of the prophet Zoroaster, articulates the perpetual struggle between the forces of good and evil—an eternal battle that spans the realms of the material and spiritual, shaping the destiny of both humanity and the universe itself.

Zoroastrianism portrays the universe as the battleground of two opposing cosmic forces. On one side stands Ahura Mazda, the supreme deity symbolizing truth, wisdom, order, and light. On the other side stands Angra Mainyu, also known as Ahriman, embodying falsehood, ignorance, chaos, and darkness.

This fundamental dualism extends beyond mere allegory; it reflects a profound belief in the reality of these opposing forces and their influence over the fabric of existence. It asserts that the struggle between good and evil is not only conceptual but also deeply woven into the very essence of the universe.

Human Agency and Moral Choice:

Zoroastrianism places human beings at the center of this cosmic drama. Individuals are seen as active participants in the struggle, wielding the power to align with either the forces of light or those of darkness through their choices and actions.

The dualistic worldview introduces a clear moral framework. Righteousness, truthfulness, compassion, and benevolence are aligned with Ahura Mazda, while deceit, cruelty, and malevolence align with Angra Mainyu.

Zoroastrianism emphasizes the profound responsibility of humans to actively choose the path of good and contribute to the eventual triumph of truth over falsehood. While the cosmic battle rages on, Zoroastrianism envisions a future in which the forces of good will ultimately prevail. Ahura Mazda will triumph over Angra Mainyu, bringing about a cosmic renewal marked by harmony, order, and the defeat of evil.

Zoroastrian eschatology includes a day of judgment when all souls will be assessed based on their choices and actions. The righteous will be rewarded with eternal happiness, while the wicked will face retribution.

The dualistic worldview offers a clear distinction between right and wrong, providing a foundation for ethical living and social responsibility. Zoroastrianism's belief in the ultimate triumph of good provides a source of hope and resilience in the face of adversity.

Fire Temples and Rituals in Zoroastrianism: The Sacred Flame of Devotion

Central to Zoroastrian worship and spiritual practice are fire temples, sacred spaces where the eternal flame burns as a symbol of divine presence, purity, and the eternal struggle between good and evil. These temples, rooted in the heart of Zoroastrianism, provide a haven for reverence, connection, and the perpetuation of ancient rituals that honor the cosmic forces and guide followers toward righteousness.

The Significance of Fire:

Fire is regarded as a sacred element in Zoroastrianism, representing the divine light, truth, and the illuminating power of Ahura Mazda. It is believed to have the capacity to purify, cleanse, and transform matter. It is a medium through which offerings are made to the divine realm.

The fire's perpetual burning mirrors the cosmic battle between good and evil, serving as a reminder of the ongoing conflict between the forces of light and darkness.

Fire Temples: Sanctuaries of Devotion:

Zoroastrian fire temples are characterized by architectural precision and symbolism. The sacred fire is enshrined in an inner chamber called the "Atash Kadeh," often situated on an elevated platform.

The Atash Kadeh is attended to by priests who ensure its continuous burning. Devotees gather in these temples for communal worship, prayers, and rituals.

Worship and Rituals:

Zoroastrians offer various substances to the fire, such as sandalwood, myrrh, and incense, symbolizing devotion, reverence, and connection with the divine.

Prayer is central to Zoroastrian practice. Devotees recite the Avesta, the holy scripture of Zoroastrianism, while facing the sacred fire.

Festivals and Ceremonies:

- **Nowruz:** Zoroastrian New Year, known as Nowruz, is celebrated with special rituals in fire temples. The fire is an integral part of the purification ceremonies during this festival.
- **Sadeh:** Sadeh, a mid-winter festival, involves the lighting of bonfires as a symbolic act of dispelling darkness and celebrating the triumph of light.

Flame of Connection and Continuity:

Fire temples and rituals in Zoroastrianism serve as a sacred bridge that connects devotees with the divine, the eternal struggle between good and evil, and the timeless traditions of their faith. The sacred flame represents the enduring spirit of Zoroastrianism—a flame that kindles devotion, purifies intentions, and ignites the soul's quest for alignment with the divine order.

As the fire burns in these temples, it embodies the timeless teachings of Zoroaster, resonating with the call to live a life of righteousness, wisdom, and devotion to the eternal light of Ahura Mazda.

Zoroastrianism's Influence on Persian History and Thought: Shaping a Nation's Identity and Values

Zoroastrianism has indelibly shaped the course of Persian history, culture, and thought. Its profound influence resonates in every facet of Persian identity, from governance and ethics to literature and art, casting a timeless shadow that continues to guide the nation's trajectory.

Foundations of Persian Civilization:

Teachings of moral rectitude, truthfulness, and devotion to the cosmic battle between good and evil became intrinsic to the Persian identity. The values it propagated helped shape a cohesive society and provided a moral compass for the rulers and subjects alike.

Zoroastrianism was the official state religion of the Achaemenid Empire, which embraced its principles of justice, benevolence, and religious tolerance. This ethos influenced the empire's administration and its outlook on governance.

Ethical and Philosophical Contributions:

Zoroastrianism's belief in a benevolent and wise supreme deity, Ahura Mazda, fostered an ethical framework that emphasized the pursuit of truth, righteousness, and ethical conduct. These principles permeated Persian philosophy, enriching discourses on ethics and justice.

The concept of dualism, rooted in Zoroastrianism's vision of cosmic struggle, found resonance in Persian thought. It shaped discussions on the interplay between opposing forces and the quest for equilibrium.

Impact on Persian Literature and Art:

Zoroastrian scriptures, including the Avesta, played a foundational role in shaping Persian literature. The themes of cosmic battle, moral choices, and the quest for enlightenment permeated epic narratives, poetry, and prose.

The sacred fire, central to Zoroastrian worship, became a powerful symbol in Persian art and architecture. Fire temples, torchlit ceremonies, and the representation of flames in art reflected Zoroastrianism's influence on aesthetic expressions.

Zoroastrianism's legacy remains a point of pride for modern Iranians, symbolizing the rich heritage of their nation and offering a connection to their ancestral roots. The inclusive nature of Zoroastrianism's values continues to influence contemporary discussions on tolerance, coexistence, and interfaith dialogue.

Modern Challenges and Revival Efforts of Zoroastrianism: Navigating a Changing Landscape

Zoroastrianism, with its rich heritage and ancient legacy, faces a spectrum of modern challenges that test its resilience and adaptability. As the world evolves and societies transform, the followers of this ancient faith are confronted with the task of preserving their traditions while navigating the complexities of contemporary life. Amidst these challenges, dedicated efforts for revival are emerging, breathing new life into the teachings and practices of Zoroastrianism.

One of the most pressing challenges is the small number of Zoroastrians worldwide. The global community has experienced a decline in numbers due to factors such as emigration, interfaith marriages, and low birth rates.

Engaging younger generations and instilling a sense of pride and connection to their Zoroastrian heritage is essential for the faith's survival. The challenge lies in striking a balance between preserving tradition and embracing modernity.

However, some ongoing revival efforts include:

- **Education and Awareness:** Initiatives to educate both Zoroastrian youth and the general public about the faith's history, teachings, and contributions help foster a sense of identity and pride.
- **Community Building:** Strengthening community bonds through social events, gatherings, and support networks can counter the isolation that sometimes accompanies small religious communities.
- **Cultural Celebrations:** Reviving and celebrating traditional festivals and rituals can rekindle a sense of communal belonging and help pass down cultural practices to younger generations.

The challenges facing Zoroastrianism in the modern era are not insurmountable obstacles but rather opportunities for growth, adaptation, and revival. Efforts to preserve the teachings, values, and cultural richness of Zoroastrianism are being spearheaded by passionate individuals and organizations. By embracing change while staying rooted in their heritage, Zoroastrians are navigating a path that respects tradition while embracing the dynamism of the present. The future of Zoroastrianism is being shaped by these dedicated efforts to ensure that its ancient flame continues to burn brightly in the modern world.

Conclusion

The threads of belief and practice across religions weave together a vibrant mosaic of human spirituality. Amidst the diversity, there are common threads that bind us—shared values, moral principles, and a universal quest for meaning. As we step back to reflect on this intricate weave, we uncover not only the richness of human faith but also the potential for greater understanding and unity.

- **Ethical Compass:** Across religious traditions, we find a moral compass that points toward virtues such as compassion, justice, love, and humility. These shared values transcend cultural boundaries and guide individuals toward righteous living.
- **Human Dignity:** The sanctity of human life and the inherent worth of every individual are celebrated in various ways within different faiths. This shared reverence for human dignity underscores the importance of compassion and empathy.
- **Community and Connection:** The idea of belonging to a larger community, whether it's a congregation, a sangha, or an ummah, is a universal aspect of religious life. These communities provide support, nurture social bonds, and offer spaces for spiritual growth.
- **Interconnectedness:** Beneath the surface of these diverse rituals, symbols, and doctrines, lies a recognition of the interconnectedness of all life. Many religions teach the importance of harmonious relationships with both humanity and the natural world.
- **Seeking Transcendence:** The search for transcendence—whether it's through prayer, meditation, service, or

self-reflection—resonates across religious boundaries. This pursuit underscores the universal human longing for meaning beyond the material realm.

The Importance of Religious Tolerance and Understanding in a Globalized World:

In an interconnected world, where cultures collide and borders blur, understanding and tolerance are paramount. Religions that once existed within geographical confines now intermingle, requiring us to appreciate the nuances of beliefs different from our own.

Religious intolerance often stems from ignorance and misunderstanding. Knowledge is the antidote—learning about other faiths dispels stereotypes and nurtures a sense of respect for differing perspectives.

Religion has immense potential to be a bridge for peace, fostering understanding and cooperation among diverse communities. When we understand that our values are often more similar than they are different, the potential for harmony increases.

Embracing Unity and Diversity:

As we reflect on the world's religions, we encounter a collage of humanity's most profound beliefs and aspirations. Amidst the intricate designs and vibrant colors, we see the reflection of our shared humanity—a reminder that our paths may diverge, but our collective journey is guided by a universal search for truth, meaning, and connection. In a world that grows smaller by the day, the importance of religious tolerance and understanding cannot be overstated. By celebrating our common threads and respecting our differences, we embrace the potential to weave a tapestry of global harmony, where diversity is celebrated and unity is cherished.

References

Allabout. (2014). Three Hundred Year Of The Khalsa - Gateway To Sikhism. *Gateway to Sikhism.* https://www.allaboutsikhs.com/sikh-literature/sikhism-articles/three-hundred-year-of-the-khalsa/

Bryan, R. (2019, May 25). *What are the core beliefs of Reform Judaism? – handlebar-online.com.* https://www.handlebar-online.com/other/what-are-the-core-beliefs-of-reform-judaism/

Deepak Sharma, & Deepak Sharma. (2023). Temples that Take Your Breath Away: Top 5 Must-Visit Temples in India. *Since Independence.* https://www.sinceindependence.com/religion/temples-that-take-your-breath-away-top-5-must-visit-temples-in-india

Fuyu, & Fuyu. (2023, September 15). Who is Dogen Zenji? | Zen-Buddhism.net. *Zen Buddhism | SIMPLE WISDOM FOR HAPPY LIVING.* https://www.zen-buddhism.net/who-is-dogen-zenji/

Jessj. (2023, March 22). Yoga and Meditation in Recovery - Mindfulness-Based Interventions. *All Points North.* https://apn.com/blog/2022/01/19/yoga-and-meditation-in-recovery/

Knight, H. (2023). Sikh Traditions | Full List & Guide (Customs and Practices). *Faith Inspires.* https://faithinspires.org/sikh-traditions/

Ktucker. (2020). Why we celebrate: Hanukkah. *Root and Vine.* https://rootandvinenews.com/why-we-celebrate-hanukkah/

Martin, L. H., & Wiebe, D. (2013). The Scientific Study of Religion: Two case studies, one response. *Method & Theory in the Study of Religion, 25*(4–5), 478–485. https://doi.org/10.1163/15700682-12341310

Patil, H. (2023). Discovering Oneness Through The MahaVakya, Ekam Sat & Sab Ka Malik Ek. *Shirdi Sai Baba Stories.* https://www.shirdisaibabastories.org/2023/04/sab-ka-malik-ek/

Pixoram. (n.d.). *Islamic Wall Art: Canvas prints for your spiritual space.* https://pixoram.com/collections/islamic

Rhedrig, & Rhedrig. (2023). 10 Surprising benefits of meditation and mindfulness for your physical and mental health. *www.upcomingswatch.com.* https://www.upcomingswatch.com/2023/01/10-surprising-benefits-of-meditation.html

Sanchi Great Stupa. (n.d.). http://sanchi.org/sanchi-great-stupa.html

Sebastian, P. (2023, May 25). *Unlocking Inner Bliss: The power and Importance of Samyama Meditation - CherishSisters.* CherishSisters. https://cherishsisters.com/unlocking-inner-bliss-the-power-and-importance-of-samyama-meditation/

Semwal, S. (2023, February 28). Difference between Jainism and Buddhism - Edukar India. *Edukar India.* https://edukar.in/difference-between-jainism-and-buddhism/

Venngage. (n.d.). Diwali template. *Venngage.* https://venngage.com/templates/invitations/diwali-template-e44bfbbd-ca40-4cca-94c5-1ce5fc8ceee3

Verma, M. (2023). 10 Lines Essay On Hajj In English For Students. *English Summary.* https://englishsummary.com/10-lines-essay-on-hajj-in-english-for-students/

Webmaster. (2015, December 3). Strength In Faith: Muslim students remain grounded in faith. *The Ithacan.* https://theithacan.org/life-culture/strength-in-faith-muslim-students-remain-grounded-in-faith/

Zerkalenkov, Z. (n.d.). *3 Chinese Concepts to Help You Live a Happier Life | By Zhenya Zerkalenkov | Tealfeed.* Tealfeed. https://tealfeed.com/3-chinese-concepts-help-live-happier-eazaq

Printed in Great Britain
by Amazon